Changabang

Changabang

Chris Bonington
Martin Boysen
Alan Hankinson
Dougal Haston
Balwant Sandhu
Doug Scott

1976
OXFORD UNIVERSITY PRESS
New York

Acknowledgements

This book has six authors. Perhaps it should have been sub-titled 'Six Authors in search of a Character'. Each writer is indicated at the start of each of his contributions, usually by Christian name but Lt. Col. Balwant Sandhu by his nickname 'Ballu' and I by mine which is 'Hank'. Wherever no name is given, the responsibility is mine alone. The responsibility for the assembly and the editing is also mine.

We owe our collective thanks to the many people and groups whose generous help made the expedition possible, especially to Air India and the Indian Mountaineering Foundation who between them enabled us to cut our transport and administrative costs to the minimum. And we remember with pleasure as well as gratitude the host of people who made us warmly welcome in India, particularly the President of the I.M.F., Mr. H. C. Sarin, and Capt. and Mrs. D. F. Robbins of the British High Commission in New Delhi.

Finally, my thanks must go to the wives of the British climbers for their heart-searchings in the penultimate chapter and to my own wife who, as ever, did all the typing and most of the secretarial work and kept a closely critical eye on the book at every stage.

Alan Hankinson

First published in the U.S.A.
by Oxford University Press Inc. 1976

ISBN 0 19 519836 0

Printed in Great Britain

Preface

Changabang had its own special beauty. It was one of the most satisfying and enjoyable mountain experiences any of us had ever had. There is the mountain itself, a shark's tooth of pale grey granite cleaving the sky at the head of the Rhamani Glacier. It's not a public mountain in the way of the Eiger North Wall or even Everest where the whole world can follow progress through the eyes of the media. Few people have seen Changabang. Hidden away on the edge of the Nandi Devi Sanctuary, it cannot be seen from any road or path or even high grazing Alp. The region where it stands, the Garhwal, is one of the most dramatically beautiful of the Himalayas, a place of awesome gorges, rich vegetation, many-coloured Alpine flowers, jagged granite mountains.

The way we climbed Changabang was especially satisfying. We started out as two separate parties of Indians and Britons, with myself the only link between the two. I had been fortunate enough to meet and climb with all the Indian climbers the previous summer. But in the course of the expedition we merged into a single group, friendship and mutual respect growing as we got to know and understand each other better. I saw new facets of my own close friends as well as my new friends from India.

Six of the eight climbers were able to reach the summit, climbing together as a single party, all deeply committed to the climb, without the aid of high-altitude porters, without any kind of back-up team beyond Advance Base Camp. It made for a very intense and exciting experience.

We have tried to reflect this in the way we have told the story. Alan Hankinson, who was with us on the South Face of Annapurna as a member of the Independent Television News team, came out with us for a month and has held the story together, but all of us—even our wives—have contributed our own impressions of the climb and our relationships with each other. In making this mosaic I hope we have succeeded in giving a broader picture of a magnificent mountain region and our experience there.

Chris Bonington

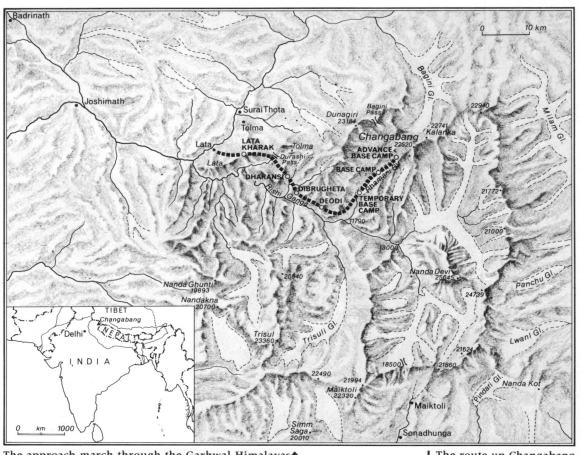

The approach march through the Garhwal Himalayas↑

↓ The route up Changabang

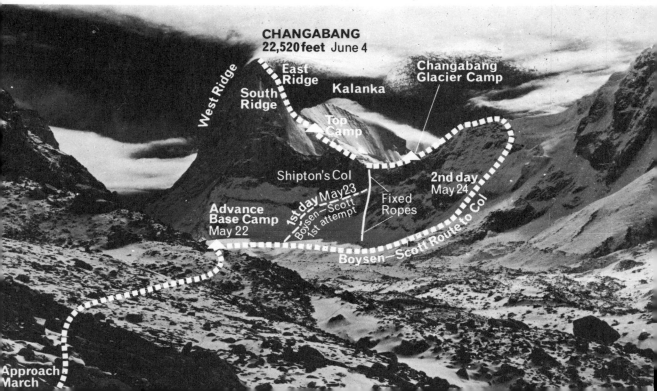

CHANGABANG
22,520 feet June 4

West Ridge

East Ridge

South Ridge

Kalanka

Changabang Glacier Camp

Top Camp

Shipton's Col

1st day May23
Boysen–Scott
1st attempt

Fixed Ropes

2nd day May 24

Advance Base Camp May 22

Boysen–Scott Route to Col

Approach March

Contents

Glossary of Terms

abseil   descend by means of a *fixed rope*.

à cheval   climb a narrow *ridge* by sitting astride it.

aiguille   a rock pinnacle.

anchor   see *belay*.

arête   a narrow *ridge*.

artificial climbing   climbing by the direct use of modern aids such as *pitons, nuts, slings, étriers,* etc.

belay (*or anchor*)   make a stance safe by securing yourself to the rock or ice.

bivouac   a night out in the mountains without a tent.

col   a mountain pass; the lowest point on a *ridge* between two peaks.

cornice   an overhanging lip of snow.

couloir   a gully.

crampons   a steel device with sharp spikes which attaches beneath the boots for climbing ice or hard snow.

descendeur   metal clip which attaches to the *fixed rope* to aid an *abseil*.

duvet   a down jacket.

étrier   a short, portable ladder.

fixed rope   rope clipped to a *piton* and left hanging down to help subsequent ascents and descents.

front-point   climb on the front, forward-projecting points of the *crampons*.

gendarme   a rock tower on a *ridge*.

head wall   steep section at top of a route.

Hiebler   metal clamp for ascending *fixed rope*.

ice screw   *piton* with thread for screwing into hard ice.

jumar   metal clamp for ascending *fixed rope*. A ratchet permits it to slide up the rope but not down; easier to use than the *Hiebler* but not so reliable on icy rope. On easy-angled slopes a single jumar is used, connected to the climber's waist. On steeper ground one jumar connects to his waist, another to a *sling* which goes under one boot.

karabiner   metal snap-like to clip together the climber, ropes, *pitons, slings,* etc.

leading through   the practice, with two climbers roped together, of taking turns to lead.

moraine   rocky debris alongside a glacier.

nut   metal chocks which slot into cracks to protect the climber.

overhang   section of cliff which leans out beyond the vertical.

peg   see *piton*.

pitch   section of a climb between *belay* points.

piton metal nail hammered into cracks to afford a *belay*.
ridge the line at which two faces of a mountain meet.
serac tower of ice.
sling loop of tape or rope.

To the mountaineers and
the mountain people
of India

1. Beginnings

1. Getting involved

AS FAR AS I was concerned it all happened with bewildering suddenness.

Chris Bonington and I were climbing a route called 'The Shroud' on Troutdale Pinnacle in Borrowdale just after Easter. The weather was brilliant and Chris, who is a conversational climber, was enthusing in his usual way for all the world as if he had never been on a steep rock route in the Lake District before. I was at the first belay point, clipped into a couple of piton slings and paying out the rope as he set about the second pitch, when he began to talk about Changabang. I knew he was off to the Himalayas again at the end of the month, but nothing more.

'The trouble is,' he called down casually as he scanned the rock above for his next moves, 'I don't feel much like sitting down at the end of it all to churn out another bloody expedition book. I've done two in the last four years and that's quite enough. I'm getting stale.'

'I'll write the book,' I said, without thinking.

'You would?' He stopped climbing for a moment. 'That'd be great!'

'Sure,' I said, beginning to think about it now, 'but I ought to come too, you know—to get to know everyone properly and find out what the mountain's like, and I'm not sure I can get the time off at this kind of notice.'

'Don't worry about that. It can be fixed all right.'

Chris enjoys fixing almost as much as he enjoys climbing. To him an obstructive official or some apparently intractable problem of logistics or administration represents a stimulating challenge, and the harder the challenge the more fiercely he is prepared to persuade and cajole, bully and, if necessary, simply bore people into compliance.

Nine times out of ten he gets his way in the end. Exactly two weeks later, still wondering what had hit me, I was on board an Air India jumbo jet bound for New Delhi *en route* for Changabang.

2. 'Another bloody expedition book'

In the end I could not write the whole book because I could only get one month's leave of absence from my job and the climb was bound to take longer. So it was decided that we would all collaborate—each of the four British climbers and the Indian leader would deal with incidents that had involved or interested him and I would fill in the gaps and stitch it all together to make, we hoped, a coherent story. Four of us, after all, had already produced books about climbing and two of us, Chris and Doug Scott, were keen and experienced photographers, so we might hope that the pictures would carry us through when the words failed.

The idea was to create something that would not be just 'another bloody expedition book' describing in laborious detail the movement of men and supplies up the mountain, but a more impressionistic account which tried to convey something of what it feels like to be part of a medium-sized, mixed-nationality expedition in the Himalayas and to climb a hard route at a high altitude. Seeing it through six separate pairs of eyes might help to build up a truer picture, more rounded and more varied and more interesting. Changabang, where the emphasis was on the climbing and the personalities of the climbers rather than administration and logistics, was an ideal subject for such treatment. That, at any rate, was the intention. This book is the result.

2. The Climb and the Climbers

UNTIL RECENTLY the conquest of the high summits of the Himalayas was more a matter of endurance and determination and the ability to organise the ferrying of supplies than of pure climbing. The aim was simply to get at least two men to the top and safely down again. When men first approach a very high mountain they naturally look for the easiest way up it, and it was in this way, in the 1950s and 1960s, that the highest mountains of all—the 8000-metre peaks—were all conquered.

The next logical stage was to look for harder routes. Some went for the steeper faces of already-conquered giants—the Rupal Face of Nanga Parbat, Annapurna South Face, and the South-West Face of Everest, the latest of a long line of the 'last great challenges' that have punctuated mountaineering history. Others sought out lesser but more demanding mountains—untouched summits, between 20 000 and 25 000 feet, which were made interesting by the fact that there was no obvious or easy way up them. There are hundreds of such peaks in the Himalayas. Changabang was one of them—22 520 feet high—and one of the most attractive. It offered the chance to apply modern techniques of hard climbing, developed in the European Alps over several decades, at higher altitudes than Europe can provide.

The Changabang expedition would be medium-sized and, by Himalayan standards, comparatively inexpensive. It would be bi-national, four British climbers and four Indian.

Recent precedents in international mountaineering were not encouraging. In 1971 the American, Norman Dyhrenfurth, took a mixed bag of nationalities to attempt the South-West Face of Everest, but his struggle to get them to work as a team through high-minded idealism and democratic leadership foundered on ancient, deep-rooted suspicions and rivalries between the Latins and the Anglo-Saxons. And the year after that Dr. Herrligkoffer's expedition to the same Face established that it was almost as difficult to get happy co-operation between Germans and British.

The auguries for Changabang, though, seemed more promising. For one thing, it would be a much smaller and less complicated expedition. For another, there would be little or no language problem—with one exception, all the Indian climbers spoke good English. Furthermore, Chris Bonington had already met the Indian climbers the year before and had climbed with some of them on a mountain called Brammah Peak.

Finally, and perhaps most important of all, the Indians were fully and modestly aware that when it came to hard technical climbing on steep rock or ice they would have to follow the lead of the British.

'We are toddlers in the world of modern hard mountaineering. We are just beginners—we have everything to learn.' One of the distinguished veterans of Indian climbing said this to me at a cocktail party in Delhi before we set off for Changabang. 'Even when an Indian expedition put nine men on the summit of Everest and they came back national heroes, I warned them not to be too cocksure. For they had gone up Everest the easy way. As far as real hard climbing goes, the way it's done on the big walls in the Alps, we Indians are still nothing more than toddlers.' It was an important aim of the Indian involvement in Changabang that some of their leading mountaineers should become acquainted with the latest techniques and equipment.

The Indian leader on Changabang, para-colonel Balwant Sandhu, reflected on the purposes of the expedition:

> During a climbing season an average European climber does a lot of artificial climbing; an Indian hardly any. To make a marriage of classical and artificial techniques, two British and six Indians climbed together on the unclimbed Brammah in 1973. Nick Estcourt and Chris Bonington reached the summit. And now we are off to Changabang. Why Changabang? 22 520 feet is not all that impressive in the Himalayas. The manner these feet stand atop one another is. Top 5000 feet of all three faces are mostly vertical and occasionally overhung. The three ridges loop off the top like clotheslines—knife-edged and steep.
>
> Would this be a fit challenge for British climbers planning to attempt Everest South-West Face in '75? Would it be the toughest technical climb attempted by the Indian members? The answer to these questions is perhaps the answer to the question why?

The British team that Bonington assembled was well-suited to its job. He himself was the current big name in big expeditions and already on friendly terms with the Indians. Dougal Haston was famous for his almost unparalleled drive in atrocious conditions at high altitudes. Martin Boysen was known as one of the best free climbers, able to surmount extremely difficult routes, especially rock routes, without resorting to artificial aids. And Doug Scott was similarly renowned as a specialist in modern artificial methods, the use of pitons and slings and étriers to force a way up routes so holdless and steep that they cannot be tackled in any other way. They knew each other well, had climbed together before, respected each other and knew they could get along.

They had other things in common. They were all in their thirties and

1. **Back at Base Camp after the climb.** *Back row, left to right:* Kiran, Martin Tashi, Doug, Dougal, Ujagar Singh. *Front row, left to right:* Chris, DJ Singh, Ballu.

married; all fairly well educated and independent-minded and articulate and agnostic; not great club men, except for Doug, but all reasonably companionable; all were capable of total relaxation when there was nothing to be done; and all of them, in the manner of modern British climbers, inclined to sandals and jeans and general sloppiness in their personal appearance. They were hairy men. There were three beards among the five of us and all five heads carried a luxuriant growth of hair falling to well below the regulation nape of the neck.

The sight of this party arriving in Delhi at the start of the trip must have been unnerving to the Indian mountaineers. They are drawn, for the most part, from the officer ranks of the Indian services. They wear well-cut suits and stand erect and speak almost impeccable English in almost impeccable public school accents, though with an endearing way of using out-dated upper-class slang expressions and getting them slightly wrong. They are correct and charming, hospitable and impressively well-informed. If the appearance of the British contingent horrified them, as it must have done, they were too well-mannered to let it show.

In Delhi we stayed at the Defence Services' Officers' Institute, and some of the non-mountaineering residents clearly suspected that the place had been invaded by a gang of hippie squatters. But they took no steps, except to ask, courteously but firmly, that if we wanted to go swimming in their pool, would we please wear bathing caps as the Sikhs did.

People outside the climbing world or on the fringes of it are always looking for the common denominator among climbers, as if there were some mystery ingredient which would explain why they take their pleasure in a way that seems, to the majority of mankind, uncomfortable and dangerous and altogether unattractive. There must be, they seem to think, some special and unusual characteristic, common to climbers and denied to others, to account for their otherwise unaccountable pastime. If there is such a thing, no-one has yet succeeded in finding it. There are, of course, certain basic qualifications—a degree of physical fitness, a sense of balance, an urge to adventure—but these qualities are common enough and beyond this climbers seem to be as varied and as various as any other group of people. Some of them are tall and some are small; many are slim but some are not; there are moody introverted climbers and gangs of rumbustious rowdies; it is a sport that has fascinated humanity from the ignorant, aggressive lout, swilling his beer and swinging his fists, to men of high intellect and culture and fastidious taste—poets and scientists, eminent lawyers and Cabinet Ministers, even leader-writers for *The Guardian*. And most climbers, like most other people in other fields of life and sport, operate somewhere between the extremes and are indistinguishable from ordinary men and women who would never dream of going climbing.

A closer look at the British climbers who went to Changabang shows just how different men can be who share the same passion.

1. Chris Bonington

The five of us were having lunch one day at the Officers' Institute in Delhi, ranged along either side of a long table, when we were joined by a senior Indian officer who was also a mountaineer of some eminence. I think that at first he took me for the leader of our contingent, presumably because I looked a little more venerable and respectable than the others. So I put the record straight and introduced him to Chris who was sitting opposite. 'My goodness me,' the officer said, 'you are the leader? Why are you not sitting at the head of the table?' It was said with a smile but I suspect it was meant seriously too. If he had been the expedition leader, he would have been sitting at the head of the table.

Chris takes his leadership more democratically. For one thing he likes to choose his companions from among his old friends. For another he knows that any attempt to lean on them too heavily would invite a very dusty and forthright response. So he wears his authority as lightly as he can, and reaches decisions, as much as possible, by discussion and consensus. He operates like the chairman of a committee rather than a commanding officer. And it works; he usually gets his way; his expeditions are usually successful; and, most remarkable of all, when they are over the members are still talking to each other and to Chris.

He has made himself one of the best-known mountaineers in the history of the sport. His lectures fill the Festival Hall and overflow lesser auditoria. Millions of those who prefer their Bank Holiday thrills to come vicariously have watched him, from the safety of their television sets, climbing in the Cheddar Gorge, in Glencoe and on the Old Man of Hoy. His books—four so far, including an autobiography published when he was thirty-one—sell by the tens of thousands. In his role as photographer-journalist he has been assigned by the *Daily Telegraph Magazine* to cover a variety of adventure stories—a volcano in Ecuador, hunting with the Canadian Eskimos, shooting the rapids of the Blue Nile in an inflatable rubber boat, trudging the endless roads of South America with Sebastian Snow. He has won the ultimate accolades of the British media—played panel games on television and a selection of records on Roy Plomley's radio desert island. It is a remarkable achievement by any standards, particularly remarkable for a man who, up to the age of twenty-seven, had known repeated failure.

He failed to get to university. For reasons which have never been made clear, he got no marks at all in one of his A Level English papers. So he joined the R.A.F. for his national service and became one of the most dangerously incompetent trainee pilots they have ever had. He once narrowly missed a petrol tanker while taxi-ing his small plane along the runway. So he transferred to the army and was commissioned into the Royal Tank Regiment, only to realise after a few years that he was not cut out for the closed world of regimental soldiering. So he left the forces and joined Van den Berghs, the margarine division of Unilevers, as a management trainee. In six months as their representative in the Hampstead area he lost their accounts with a dozen grocers and gained not a single new one. When he asked them for leave of absence to join an expedition to South America, the opportunity must have seemed heaven-sent to Van den Berghs. They told him he had to choose between margarine and mountaineering. He chose to climb. It was a brave decision. He had £50 in the bank and had just got married and it meant several years of hardship for him and Wendy. But it was inevitable.

For more than ten years Chris had known that his heart lay irretrievably in the mountains. It began when he was sixteen and a friend took him to Harrison's Rocks, forty miles south of London: 'I felt a sympathy with the rock; I found that my body somehow slipped into balance naturally, without any conscious thought on my part. There was not much height to worry about, for the crag was only thirty feet, but what there was did not worry me; if anything, I found it stimulating. I knew that I had found a pursuit that I loved, that my body and my temperament seemed designed for it, and that I was happy.'

His climbing progressed quickly, first in Snowdonia, then in Scotland and the Alps with Hamish MacInnes, then the Dolomites with Gunn Clark. In 1960 he went to the Himalayas with a joint services expedition and reached the summit of Annapurna Two. The next year he was on the ill-tempered expedition to Nuptse, then, with Don Whillans and Ian Clough, climbed the Central Pillar of Frêney in the Alps. The year after that, the summer season that followed his resignation from Van den Berghs, his Alpine exploits made him famous well beyond mountaineering circles. On the North Wall of the Eiger he and Don Whillans rescued Brian Nally after his friend, Barry Brewster, had been killed by falling rocks high up on the face. He climbed the Walker Spur with Ian Clough. Then, again with Ian, he conquered the North Wall of the Eiger. It was the first British ascent and his lectures about it earned enough money to take him and Wendy out to the Central Tower of Paine in Patagonia.

He was well-known by now but far from well-off and he recognised the need to acquire new skills. Most professional mountaineers earn their living by teaching and guiding but Chris knew himself well enough to realise that he was too impatient and ambitious to settle for this. So he learned photography and polished his writing, and, slowly at first, the journalistic commissions came. In the mid-'60s he joined the ranks of the TV climbers. And in 1970 he embarked on a new career, expedition leading. The ascent of the South Face of Annapurna was more than a mountaineering success; it established Chris as an outstanding leader— a fine and experienced all-round climber; a capable organiser with a sharp eye for the main chance and a persuasive tongue, a natural PR man able to tell the same story to a succession of reporters without losing any freshness or enthusiasm; and a fair but forceful leader on the mountain itself. Annapurna was not without its frictions but compared to most other ventures of that size it was virtually trouble-free. Two years later on the South-West Face of Everest, he showed the same qualities and an extra one, dogged determination in the face of terrible set-backs and hardships.

Success brought Chris Bonington fame and money and also criticism. The climbing community in Britain is comparatively small and highly competitive. Its members pride themselves on being outspoken, in pubs and club huts and in the pages of their magazines. For some of them Chris has introduced too intense an element of commercialism into the sport. To others it seems that he has come to dominate the expedition field to the exclusion of equally-deserving people. There are good answers to such charges. Chris is by no means the only climber who lives by climbing and it is hard to see any sensible objection to it. 'Happy is the man,' says Professor Higgins in *Pygmalion*, 'who can make a living by his hobby'—and if Chris has any special quality it must be that he makes a rather better living than most and in a more interestingly varied way. Nor does he, in fact, hog the expedition field. There is plenty of scope for anyone able to deploy the same kind of skill and application.

Much of the resentment that Chris arouses can be explained by envy. But some of it at any rate is provoked by his nature. He is a very ambitious man, driving and competitive. He hates losing at anything, even Scrabble. He likes money and making it and knows his value in the market. He is passionately interested in himself, constantly analysing his motives and justifying his actions and confessing his faults. In conversation and in his writings, he is self-revealing. He is a very complicated person indeed.

It would be surprising, with his background, if he were not. His childhood was virtually fatherless. His father, a journalist, left home soon after Chris was born and did not return. His mother had to go out to work so he was brought up initially by his grandmother, sent away to boarding school in the North of England at the age of five, then brought back to London to become the unhappy subject of a struggle between mother and grandmother. 'I suspect,' he says, 'this left me with a feeling of insecurity.' There is, furthermore, a strong family tradition of paternal restlessness. His father was a wandering adventurer. His father's father was born in Denmark, ran away to sea, carved out an exciting career in many parts of the world, and ended up as an enlightened administrator of the Andaman Islands in the Indian Ocean. He changed his name in 1914 from Bonig to the more acceptably Anglo-Saxon Bonington.

Chris is middle class by training and upbringing, the sort of man the armed forces immediately recognise as 'officer material'. He is intelligent and articulate and speaks in the standard, slightly plummy accents of the public school man. He is, and he admits it with a wry grin, a formidable rationaliser. When he has set his heart on a course of action and this happens frequently, he first persuades himself, then everyone else that what he has in mind is clearly in the best interests of all concerned. He enjoys fixing and wheeler-dealing because, like climbing, it is something he does well. If he could have found in his early twenties some line of business that engaged his whole attention and energy, he would most likely have become by now a wealthy and powerful person.

Instead, he found climbing. 'It means more to me,' he says, 'than anything else.'

2. Dougal Haston

More than any of the others, Dougal Haston is a man who has sold his soul to mountaineering. 'From early days,' he says in his autobiography *In High Places*, 'I found that climbing was the only thing in life that gave me more than momentary satisfaction.' He has devoted his life to the pursuit of that satisfaction, from the railway bridges and rocky outcrops around his boyhood home near Edinburgh to the Western Highlands of Scotland, then to the Alps and South America, and, in recent years, to the bigger mountains of the Himalayas, Annapurna, Everest and Changabang.

He is a man of extremes and opposites. He is six feet tall but so thin that you might take him, at a casual glance, to be physically frail. In fact he commands reserves of strength and endurance that make him one of the most forceful high altitude 'goers' in the world. To see him when he is not in action, you might suppose him to be among the laziest of men— capable of prolonged inactivity, happy to lie at full stretch in the sun, reading or dozing or listening to music, taking little part in the work of planning and preparation. But on his feet, with his rucksack on his back, he is transformed. His spindly figure, bowed slightly forwards under his load, tapers down the line of his fading jeans to a pair of incongruously enormous boots, and those implacable boots move steadily up the roughest ground, rarely hesitating and never resting, inexorably widening the gap between himself and the rest of the party. 'Climbing with Dougal,' wrote the laconic 'Master', Don Whillans, after their successful partnership on Annapurna South Face, 'was like having a greyhound on a leash—you slipped it and watched him go.'

He keeps himself very fit. In the summer months he runs the International School of Mountaineering at Leysin in Switzerland and in Spring he teaches ski-mountaineering. He does a lot of walking too and

2. Dougal Haston

likes to get to the Mediterranean coast for a few weeks of swimming and skin-diving. And most years he spends two months or so on some big mountain expedition.

Dougal is a very private person, quiet, self-contained, introverted. You get the impression of an intense inner life, a continuous process of self-analysis, the earnest sifting of thoughts and feelings. But even in the pleasantly relaxed atmosphere of base camp, in the company of fellow-mountaineers, he does not open up. He speaks in a gentle, Scottish burr, but sparingly. If you question him, he replies carefully and frankly and to the point, but briefly. He does not initiate conversations.

His reading is formidably serious. He carried up to Changabang Base Camp a weighty American volume about the international monetary system, and some works of the German philosopher, Friedrich Nietzsche. He read philosophy at Edinburgh University for four years until his commitment in 1966 to the first direct ascent of the North Wall of the Eiger irretrievably interrupted his studies, and though he has never regretted the interruption—'What use would a degree be to me?'—he has never lost interest in the subject. Perhaps there is some clue to the basis of his motivation in the fact that he is interested in Nietzsche. The German preached the cult of 'the Superman', the great leader, the hero-figure who was noble, dominating, Spartan and cruel, who used his will to master himself and bring lesser mortals under his control. Dougal does not, overtly at any rate, regard himself as a 'Superman'. He says he is interested in Nietzsche no more and no less than in many other philosophers. But he might well have taken the German's doctrine of will power as a guiding tenet: '*I test the power of a will*,' Nietzsche wrote, 'according to the amount of resistance it can offer and the amount of pain and torture it can endure and know how to turn to its own advantage.'

Dougal, at the age of thirty-four, has mastered the varied skills and techniques of modern mountaineering. His interest now seems to lie in the harsher reaches of the sport, in those areas where the natural difficulties and dangers of climbing are intensified by exhaustion and altitude and privation and pain and the sheer scope and complication of the problems ahead, where the body goes on automatically doing the right things because of the accumulated experience of the years, but where a man's mind and will are supreme. It is a strange and rarefied form of fulfilment, but for Dougal, undoubtedly, it has become a source of joy.

His direct ascent of the Eiger was an epic of suffering and disaster. When he finally reached the summit his fingers were badly frostbitten, his face was iced up, his friend and companion on the climb, John Harlin, was dead; and Dougal wrote, 'I felt as if I had just come at last out of the darkness into the light, and the exploration of that light offered so many bewildering possibilities that my mind could scarcely cope with the contemplation of it all.'

In 1970, on Annapurna South Face he was afflicted for a time with piles but neither complained nor stopped climbing. 'I think he must have just ground them away,' said Whillans. A few weeks later he crouched at Camp Six, battered by high winds and sprindrift snow, trying to survive on snow water and porridge, a prey to self-doubt and mounting pessimism about the chances of success: 'Strange though it may seem,' he wrote afterwards, 'I was happy.'

And there was more high altitude suffering to come, on the South-West Face of Everest, first with the rancorous International Expedition in 1971, then the next year in the bitter weather of Chris Bonington's post-monsoon attempt.

On the plane flying out to India *en route* for Changabang I asked Dougal where, if he could choose from anywhere in the world, he would like to be. He paused a moment, then said, 'High up on the South-West Face of Everest. It annoys me that we didn't make it. There are terrible problems—the logistics of it all, the altitude, the weather—everything seems to conspire against you. I think more than anything else I'd like another go at that Face.'

'You actually enjoy it there?' I asked.

'I wouldn't do it if I didn't.'

The pleasure may be perverse but it is not masochistic. It is not the suffering that he relishes but his mastery over it. He likes to operate along the limits of his endurance. For Dougal, more than for anyone else I have met, mountaineering is a passion, pure, rigorous and consuming. He suggests the strength of his feeling in a passage in his autobiography describing Don Whillans and himself: 'We are clothed alike. We have the same objective. But in the mind, what a difference: the practical and the philosophical! He has a job to do and is doing it. I have a way of life to live and am living it.'

3. Doug Scott

We were warned before we set off on the approach march that there were brown bears in the forest above the Rishi Gorge and that they had a nasty way of resenting intruders. Without any kind of firearm, we could think of only one possible precaution—to let Doug Scott blaze the trail. By unanimous agreement, his thirteen-and-a-half stone of unruly black hair and bulging muscle was voted the prospect most likely to disconcert an angry bear, either by frightening it or by being recognised as something approaching kith, if not kin.

3. Doug Scott

Doug is big and burly and built, as Martin pointed out, 'like a brick shit-house.' He is also very strong and fit. He plays wing forward for a Nottingham rugger club and the sight of him pounding down the pitch towards you like a scruffy juggernaut with the ball tucked under one thick arm must be among the most unnerving experiences the game can offer.

He looks like a healthy hippie and talks like an anarchist. His face is framed by a black beard. The hair is kept out of his eyes, as often as not, by a strip of tea towel. The eyes glint with amusement behind a pair of steel-rimmed spectacles. His manner is straight-forward and down-to-earth, at first meeting almost aggressively proletarian. In every restaurant we visited in India his staccato Nottingham accents could be heard, doggedly demanding potatoes. He always got them.

Climbing did not come naturally to him. As a small boy, he says, he made the shameful discovery that most of his mates were more physically venturesome than he was. When it came to climbing trees and walls and other tests of skill and nerve that lads devise for themselves, most of them would go farther than him. He found himself returning to the spot in secret later to force himself to repeat their moves.

By the age of thirteen, though, he was scrambling and climbing regularly on Derbyshire gritstone. It was an escape from the urban grime around his home; he loved the freedom of camping, cooking rough meals on an open fire, bivouacking in caves, seeking adventures; he was, laboriously, learning to be a climber. The next year he carried a tent across Snowdonia and climbed a route on the Milestone Buttress in clinker-nailed boots. He was hooked. He abandoned his earlier obsession, long and middle distance running, and took to spending every weekend and holiday in the Pennines or the Lake District or North Wales. At sixteen he went to the Alps to fall off some of the Chamonix Aiguilles, and from then on he and his Nottingham friends went to the Alps every year for the next fifteen years.

He had done well at school, took A levels in history, geography and later in geology, and then went to Loughborough for two years' teacher training. For the next ten years he taught geography and social studies at the secondary modern school where he had been educated. But climbing and expeditions claimed more and more of his time and interest.

There can be few more devoted expedition men. In his early teens he read *Upon That Mountain* and thrilled to Eric Shipton's story of mountain exploration in the wild places of the world. Shipton became his personal hero. The Shipton way of life became Scott's. In 1962 he went with a group of Nottingham friends to the Atlas mountains of North Africa, and in the years that followed the tally of his trips multiplied fast. He went to Tibesti in Chad, to Kurdistan and the Hindu Kush, to the Alps and Norway, twice to the big blank walls of Yosemite in California, three times to Baffin Island in the Canadian Arctic, and twice in one eventful year, 1972, to Everest—before the monsoon with the disputatious German expedition led by Dr. Herrligkoffer, and after it with the storm-swept Bonington expedition.

Doug Scott is thirty-two and married. His wife, Jan, who is a teacher, and their two children see increasingly little of him. Three years ago he stopped regular teaching. He found that he could make more money as a casual labourer on building sites and needed a lot of time to research and write his book, *Big Wall Climbing*. But most of all, he wanted to be free to go on expeditions.

He could live, I suppose, without climbing, but it is clear that without the repeated and renewed challenge of hard routes in severe circumstances life would lose much of its savour and point. Extrovert, open, and high-spirited, he has nothing about him to suggest Dougal's brand of messianic intensity. But for him, too, climbing is a chosen way of life. On the Herrligkoffer expedition to Everest, Doug had a tough time. The Munich doctor disliked him from the start, presumably for his blunt, working-class ways, and tried to get rid of him. The German and Austrian climbers resented him and the other Britons, accusing Don Whillans especially of laziness and planning to snatch the summit glory. And the whole thing was so eccentrically conducted that there was little chance of success. Despite all this the quality of Doug's enjoyment shines through his published account: 'It is a sobering experience to face the harshness of the South-West Face of the highest mountain in the world, to be there in Camp 4 and have rocks perforate the sides of the box tents, to see rivers of spindrift avalanching past one's door for days on end, or to take four hours over a 1000-foot easy-angled section on fixed ropes. Climbing at 20 000 feet is vastly easier than climbing at 25 000 feet, and beyond that it's a whole new world, a world that is largely unexplored. Every day may be an adventure at a personal level. It certainly was for me.'

One phrase that is often on Doug's lips is 'total commitment'. His eyes light up when he talks about his traverse of the Kho-i-Bandaka in the Hindu Kush in 1967 when he and his Nottingham friends slept in igloos and ice caves night after night between 17 000 and 22 500 feet above sea level, and again when he describes their second trip to Baffin Island in 1972 when they humped all their gear for sixty miles across the ice to Asgard, scaled the 4000-foot East Face, then walked back again. This is what he means by 'total commitment'; getting away into wild unknown regions with a small party, seeking out situations where there is nowhere to go but on and no-one to rely on but yourselves. It is exciting while it lasts and marvellous when it is done.

By hard application, by trial and error, a good deal of fear and some failure, Doug Scott made himself a master of modern artificial rock climbing techniques. In 1969 he led the first ascent of the North-West Face Direct on Strone Ulladale on the island of Lewis in the Outer Hebrides, a big grim route on unreliable and overhanging gneiss, the sort of climb that has only been made possible by new equipment and methods, banging in metal pegs, hanging slings or étriers from them, and using the whole armoury of modern protection devices, bongs and chocks, rurps and clogs and hammers. 'Climbing up the iron men isn't everyone's cup of tea,' Scott wrote, 'but they get you into positions the likes of which free climbers will never experience. Whereas the free climber relies on the subtle shift of his body weight over his hands and feet, peg men have to use their imagination and ingenuity in the choice and placing of the pegs.' Artificial climbing is part mountaineering, part engineering. It calls for strength and patience and cunning and, most stimulating of all, a psychological adjustment to working with calm efficiency in positions that lie at and beyond the vertical. 'We have come a little nearer to this adjustment,' Scott wrote after Strone Ulladale, 'it was a unique experience.' You get the feeling that he is always learning, about his trade and about himself, and that he will never be finally satisfied because there will always be more to learn.

He learnt a lot on his two trips to Yosemite—'mind-expanding,' he says, 'milestones for me, opening up new horizons of hard free and technical climbing.' But if he is stimulated by technical developments, he is puritanical in his views about their use. He takes a strong ethical line: pegs should only be hammered home where there is no other solution; the best men will do without them, and actually take out any old ones they may find, in order to leave the rock face as undefiled as possible; wherever they can, they will place a nut into a crack and use that rather than bang in a piton.

There is a powerful element of spirituality in Doug's approach to climbing. 'The more one goes into mountains,' he says, 'the more one realises they are but a medium for exploration into oneself.' He sees expeditions as a way of escaping from urban existence with its quest for superiority and security, and its preoccupation with peripheral trivia that makes real thinking impossible.

Doug has strong views about politics and social justice. He is left-wing and radical, agnostic and anti-establishment. His sympathies are given instinctively to the poor and pushed-around people of the world. He dislikes and distrusts those who do the pushing, and he lets them know it.

4. Martin Boysen

He speaks quietly, with a slight drawl and a hint of Lancashire in the accent and a generous scattering, in climbing company at any rate, of the usual English obscenities. He likes the zanier reaches of English humour, the Goons, for example, and Bill Tidy. He sees no virtue in hard work for its own sake. 'I hate making pointless effort,' he said testily one day on the approach march when we had missed the route and had to scramble up an unpleasantly broken and vegetated slope to regain it. He is liable to sudden attacks of ill-temper but they pass quickly. He enjoyed his work, teaching biology to Manchester schoolchildren, but when he came into money—compensation for a car accident several years before—he promptly gave up his job and devoted himself instead to cheerful idleness. His normal manner, casual and relaxed and diffident, gives an impression of laziness, but the impression is misleading. In almost every way Martin Boysen would appear to be a typical modern Englishman. He is, in fact, German—by birth and early upbringing and nationality.

He was born at Alsdorf near Aachen in 1942 and one of his earliest memories is of crouching in an air-raid shelter while the R.A.F. pounded the streets above. His father, a German and a music teacher, was a reluctant recruit to the Wehrmacht and glad to be taken prisoner by the Russians because he greatly preferred their ideology to Hitler's. His mother, an Englishwoman, got work as a translator for the American

4. Martin Boysen

forces of occupation in 1945, and was not surprised to find, when she was working through the local Gestapo documents, that she and the children had been scheduled for the concentration camp. Soon after, she returned to her native Kent with her two sons, got a teaching job and settled down to await her husband's release. It was seven years before he could rejoin them.

Martin's great interest at school was natural history. He had little aptitude for ball games or athletics and preferred wandering about the countryside, observing wildlife. He spent a lot of time walking and cycling and youth hostelling about Britain. One day when he was about sixteen he found himself in the area of High Rocks near Tunbridge Wells. He watched some rock climbers in action, and they invited him to have a go on their rope. 'I found it highly exciting,' he says, 'and it seemed that I was a promising beginner. One climb led to another—an obsession had begun. A new way of life opened up and every weekend saw me packing some primitive camping gear, a pair of pumps and some hemp rope, and setting off for one or other of the outcrops.''

He quickly became what he calls 'a connoisseur of sandstone nastiness —the green slime, the fragile holds, the incredibly athletic moves, the sandiness which non-devotees not unnaturally shun.' In an article in *Mountain* magazine he wrote: 'The pleasures of climbing on sandstone are not immediate: a long finger-spraining apprenticeship has to be gone through before the real delights are opened up. It is rather like learning to play an instrument: the real satisfaction only comes after painful effort. I remember in the early days going home on a Sunday night, arms and hands seized up, unable to manipulate a knife to cut up the reheated Sunday dinner.'

He joined the Sandstone Club and began to make new routes, on High Rocks and Harrison's Rocks and on Helsby Crag above the Mersey estuary. He made the traditional progression, on to the hard gritstone routes of the Pennines, then to the bigger cliffs of the Lake District and Snowdonia where he made his name by the severity and purity of his new routes, then Scotland, the Alps and finally expeditions further afield.

Martin is six foot one inch tall, slim in build, long-limbed and loose jointed. On level ground, he has an ungainly air as if he is never quite sure how best to dispose his gangling legs and arms. But on steep rock he is a different animal. 'He is like a huge intelligent sloth,' Chris once wrote, 'conditioned to a vertical environment.'

During the two days we all spent at Josimath in the Garhwal Hills, waiting for the approach march to Changabang to get under way, we filled in time for an hour or two by bouldering—clambering about on the detached granite blocks that litter the hillside. Martin established himself straight away as the unchallenged master. Long and strong and supple, he picked out the toughest-looking routes and drifted up them without apparent effort, balancing with comfort and confidence on holds that were all but invisible, leaning wide to one side and then the other to study the way ahead, then easing himself upwards with quick but unhurried movements. He was calm and concentrated and cheerful, completely in his element. To watch him was to see rock-craft raised to the level of art, the level where the desperately difficult is made to look not only simple but graceful as well.

Twenty years ago the theory was widely held among British rock climbers that the future development of their sport lay in the hands of men of less than medium height. The evidence seemed overwhelming. Rock climbing was being carried at that time into new realms of difficulty and daring by men who were sturdy and lithe but small in stature—Joe Brown and Don Whillans, Ron Moseley and John Streetly. There was something, it seemed, in their special ratio of height to weight which gave them a crucial advantage that outweighed any benefit that might be gained from a longer reach. It is not a theory you hear much about nowadays and one of the main reasons for that is Martin Boysen. Others, incidentally, include Chris Bonington, Dougal Haston and Doug Scott, all of them at or around the six-foot mark.

There is nothing forced or intense about Martin's attitude to climbing. If there were, he would not do it. And he does it a great deal. He goes to North Wales or the Lakes most weekends and tries to get on to the Pennine gritstone near his home at least one evening each week in the summer. His forté is free climbing and he avoids as far as possible routes which entail artificial aids—partly because this involves a lot of effort, but chiefly, I suspect, because it seems unnatural. He climbs regularly in the Alps and sometimes in Norway. In 1963 he went to Patagonia with the British expedition to Cerro Torre. In 1970 he and Nick Estcourt, on the South Face of Annapurna, tackled some of the most difficult ice climbing ever undertaken at altitude, then destroyed their chances of reaching the summit by carrying loads to Camp Five at 26 000 feet until they were burnt out. Late in 1973 he went back to South America with a party attempting Torre Egger, and, though they were defeated there by continuously falling ice, he played a leading part, literally as well as metaphorically, in the conquest of the handsome rock spire across the valley called the Innominata.

Martin is not a compulsive expedition man. He climbs for fun and can enjoy himself to the limit on a thirty-foot sandstone cliff above a sewage farm. 'For me,' he says, 'sandstone climbing is much more than just good training. I derive tremendous physical enjoyment from it. After a time a sort of fitness overdrive comes in, when one is superbly fit; hard moves go with a dynamic grace which I find profoundly satisfying. I have had some of my best days climbing on sandstone, days when I have found out more about my physical limits and creative capacity to climb than I have on any other type of rock.'

He has neither need nor wish for fame or acclaim or any other of the side benefits of going on expeditions. Indeed he actively resents, sometimes with amused tolerance and sometimes with acerbity, all the trappings of publicity that attend big mountain ventures these days—the writing of books and articles, the incessant clicking and whirring of the cameras. 'If you shove that bloody thing in my face just once more,' he told a companion-photographer on the Annapurna ice ridge, 'I'll smash the lens in with my ice axe.'

Climbing may dominate Martin's leisure. It does not dominate his life. He is less obsessive about it than his fellow climbers on Changabang. And he gets more than them, I think, from the peripheral pleasures of going on an expedition—from the beauty of the views and studying the nature of the terrain, from observing the trees and flowers and birds and animals along the way and observing also the interplay of personalities among his companions, even from such mundane matters as the problem of producing an acceptable meal from limited resources. He smokes too many cigarettes and enjoys alcohol; he likes chatting and reminiscing and joking; he reads a lot, chiefly among the more entertaining classics; he loves modern jazz and classical music.

5. The Indian Team

The British team on Changabang operated like a group of climbing friends. Things were discussed openly, and if there was disagreement they were discussed heatedly too. The Indians, by contrast, operated like a small military unit. The chain of command was fixed and clear and respected. They were friendly enough among themselves for most of the time but there was never any doubt who gave the orders and who implemented them.

Their leader, co-leader with Chris of the expedition, was an impressive figure, not tall but well-proportioned and lean and strong, with mobile features and a strong baritone voice—Lieutenant-Colonel Balwant Sandhu, commanding officer of the 6th Paratroop Battalion of the Indian Army and a man born to command.

He is a man who enjoys life to the full and in many ways. He loves his soldiering, partly for the job itself—the thrills of parachuting, the pleasure of physical fitness, the challenge of controlling the volatile men of an élite corps—and partly for the opportunities it affords for the sporting life, hill-walking and shooting and fishing and horse-riding and, best of all, mountaineering. But he is a man of culture too, well-educated and widely-read, fond of the poetry of Browning and W. B. Yeats. He is an outgoing man, alert and interested and articulate. By far the most handsome man on the expedition, he was nevertheless a bachelor though undoubtedly a gay one—in the uncorrupted, heterosexual sense of the word.

From the beginning he got along easily and well with the British climbers and they quickly fell into the way of calling him by his nick-name, Ballu, which means a bear in Hindustani but which, in this case, is simply a convenient contraction of his full name. But the Indian climbers called him 'Sir' to his face and when they spoke to others they referred to him as 'the Colonel' or 'Colonel Sandhu'.

Ballu's second-in-command on the expedition was another paratroop officer, Captain Kiran Inder Kumar, a more retiring and complicated person. In the early stages he was much the busiest man on the trip, responsible for arranging all our permits and passes, buying and organising the supplies, fixing transport, sorting out the loads, hiring porters and coaxing them along—all the detailed and time-consuming work that is vital to the success of any expedition but which carries none of the glory. Busy and bustling, his clear tenor voice rising in pitch whenever the problems or the people he was dealing with began to seem intractable, he did the job conscientiously and successfully. Despite many difficulties, he got us and all the necessary equipment to Base Camp on schedule.

Kiran was a deeply religious man—unique, in this respect, on the expedition. One afternoon when a snow-storm swirled about our Temporary Base Camp, he crawled into my tent for a chat and fell into a long account of his background and beliefs. His father, an eminent and learned Hindu, had brought up the children, four boys and two girls, to be intensely devout and rigorously disciplined. Kiran advanced far on the

5. Ballu   **6. Kiran Kumar**

8. Tashi

path of yoga. He was schooled in the virtues of routine and restraint and self-control. He enjoyed cricket and wrestling at school, took an arts degree at Chandigarh University, then went into the army to astonish his comrades by taking a cold bath every day regardless of climate and altitude. Ten years or so ago, he began mountaineering. He was sustained, he told me, by the conviction that because of the piety and cleanliness of the life he had led, God was always looking over him to guard him from danger. It must be a comforting belief to take into the high mountains, but it may also be a dangerous one. Certainly Kiran was to put the matter dramatically to the test a few days later.

Ujagar Singh was the mystery man of the expedition. Small and wiry and trim, he was a soldier in the Dogra Regiment who had become an instructor at one of India's mountaineering institutes. Chris had climbed with him the year before in the Kishtwar Range just south of Kashmir and spoke highly of his climbing ability. As a person, though, it was im-

7. Ujagar Singh   9. DJ Singh

possible to get to know Ujagar. He had no English and we had no Hindustani, but even if we could have conversed together easily it is unlikely that we would have got any closer to him. He was silent and withdrawn, so self-contained that he made Dougal seem positively loquacious. He reminded me strongly of the British lance-corporals who always seemed to be in charge of my Nissen hut in my early army days—always neatly turned out, sparing but efficent in movement, for ever sorting out his equipment and cleaning it and rearranging it, rarely speaking and then only briefly, never smiling.

The fourth and final member of the Indian climbing team was a complete contrast. Sherpa Tashi Chewang was also a climbing instructor—at the Himalayan Mountaineering Institute in Darjeeling—but he spoke good English and six other languages as well, Sherpali, Nepali, Tibetan, Hindustani, Urdu and Bengali. Like the Sherpa people generally, he was cheerful and friendly, hard-working and capable. He was known to everyone simply as Tashi.

Tashi is devoted to mountaineering in all its aspects. Over the past ten years he has been on many Himalayan expeditions, as a Sherpa and as a teacher and as a climber. He developed a special interest in hard rock climbing and, in recent years, in the use of artificial techniques requiring pitons and slings. He had a formidable reputation as a determined rock climber and a hard driver of his students, a strict disciplinarian. His life of expeditions and constant travel around India to conduct climbing courses leaves him little time to be with his wife and their three daughters in Darjeeling. He told me that he is at home only forty days each year.

'Doesn't your wife complain?' I asked.

'How can she? Mountaineering is my profession. If there is no climbing, no expeditions, then there is no job, no money.'

I also asked him once if he had ever had to bivouac, sleep out, at high altitude. 'Never,' he replied, adding with a wry smile. 'Of course, I have to teach my students how to dig out an ice cave and make themselves comfortable there. I see them settled in for the night. Then I creep back to my tent.'

The remaining member of the Indian team was not a climber but the expedition doctor, Indian Army Captain Devinderjit Singh, known to everyone as D-J. When we were introduced to him in Delhi, he seemed rather forbidding, a tall full-bearded Sikh, erect in bearing, serious and apparently unbending in manner. There was no doubt that he would prove a capable doctor and that was the main thing. But he also proved to be a good hard mountain walker as well, a conscientious and inventive catering officer and a fascinating companion, interested in everything and always happy to settle down to a good, long conversation.

3. To the Garhwal

1. Farewell to Delhi

We left New Delhi in a blaze of confusion.

It was Saturday, May the 4th, Cup Final day in England and our fourth day in the city. The Indian members of the expedition who were there, Kiran and Tashi and DJ the doctor, refused to let us help with the arrangements so we devoted the time to eating and drinking, swimming and party-going, living the life of Riley Sahib.

Now, though, things were on the move. Kiran gave us our instructions. A lorry would arrive in the afternoon and we would load our personal gear, rucksacks and kitbags, on to it. At nine in the evening Kiran would collect us and take us to the bus station.

The lorry arrived on time and was soon loaded. At 8.30 we were joined by Tashi and DJ. An hour later, with still no sign of Kiran, we decided to have dinner. After that we adjourned to the bar, beginning to wonder what was causing the delay. Then Martin hurried in from the hall to say that an excited Kiran was on the phone wanting to know what we were doing. He was at the bus station and had been expecting us there for the last hour and a half. He had persuaded the driver to wait but some of the passengers were growing quite impatient. We clambered on to the lorry and rumbled off through the cool night air.

It must have been about eleven o'clock when we reached the city's main bus station. There were hundreds of people there, queuing or sleeping or drinking tea, but Kiran was not among them, nor was there any bus bound in our direction.

We conferred briefly and Chris decided to despatch DJ to inquire in all the places where Kiran might be, half a dozen spots scattered about the city. He hailed a passing rickshaw and disappeared. Chris unhitched a couple of cameras and wandered off in search of local colour. The rest of us ordered tea.

Fifteen minutes later a taxi screeched to a halt alongside our table and Kiran leapt out, followed by his brother, Colonel Kumar.

'What on earth are you doing here?' he cried.

'Waiting for you,' we replied. 'You said you'd meet us at the bus station.'

'But this is the wrong bus station. Our bus is at the Old Railway Station. We must hurry. The driver and the other passengers are becoming restless. They will not wait much longer.'

It was beginning to feel like being caught up in a Feydeau farce. We explained that we could not leave. DJ had gone off to look for Kiran and he was bound to return here in the end. We couldn't go without him. Anyway, we argued, we were very comfortable sitting on our gear in the lorry, so why not go back and tell the driver to go without us.

Kiran did not relish the prospect but in the end he went, consoling himself with the thought that at least he had not paid for the tickets.

Shortly after midnight Kiran and his brother returned, accompanied by their wives, cool and immaculate in colourful saris, and the Colonel's two young daughters. And half an hour later DJ reappeared.

We clambered off the lorry for the last time that night. The ladies produced garlands of flowers and hung them round our necks. We shook hands all round and climbed back on board.

At last we had the whole party assembled in one place and ready to go. We waited for the lorry to start. There was a pause.

'Hank,' called Doug from the front.

'Yes?'

'We can't start.'

'Why the hell not?'

'The postilion has been struck by lightning!'

But a moment later the engine spluttered into life and we moved off, followed by ragged cries of 'Goodbye!', 'Good luck!', 'Good hunting!'

Some time during all these alarums and excursions, more than four thousand miles away on the rich turf of Wembley the Cup Final had been played. It was a matter of concern to me that Liverpool should have won. But it was to be a month before I knew the reassuring result.

2. The road journey

We clattered through the night, watching the black treetops stream by in endless procession overhead and the stars disappear gradually as the sky paled towards dawn. Daylight brought heat and dust and crowded roads. We travelled east-north-east across the plains, through the holy city of Hardwar and on to the holy city of Rishikesh, bestriding the Ganges like an oriental Brighton, its many-coloured, fantastically-shaped temples jumbled together along each side of the wide river, its narrow streets alive with tourists and touts and pilgrims.

Beyond Rishikesh the road followed the river, twisting and turning interminably, gradually gaining height among the steep forest-covered hills. It was a bumpy, low-gear journey through a landscape that was almost monotonously dramatic. The slow ascent continued for a hundred miles and more. There were places where you could lean out from the

top of the lorry and look almost vertically down to the foaming waters of
the river, a thousand feet below. Every now and then we came across
working parties repairing the ravages of rockfalls and landslips and
erosion. And all the way the same signs, painted on rocks above the
road, repeated the same injunctions—'Safety Saves', and 'Horn Please'
just before a blind corner, and 'Thank You' a few yards beyond it. In
the later stages we had to stop several times at army check-points where
the signs said 'No foreigners beyond here', and we would get out to
stretch our legs while Kiran cleared our passports and permits with the
guard commander. We were entering a strategically-sensitive area, the
Tibetan border region which had been closed to non-Indians ever since
the Chinese invasion of 1962.

Josimath is the last town before the high mountains. Some 7000 feet
above the plains, it looks across a wide valley to a panorama of grey,
conical peaks, clad in conifers and shrubs, with higher rock and ice
mountains looming beyond them, all hazy in the prevailing dust cloud.

Here we met the last two members of the party, Ballu, the Indian
co-leader, fresh from guarding Pakistani prisoners-of-war in Agra, and
the unobtrusive Ujagar Singh. We stayed two days, reading and bouldering and getting to know Ballu while Kiran supervised the final arrangements. The only serious problem concerned our butane gas, needed for
cooking at the higher camps because it is much lighter to carry than
kerosene. The gas had been shipped out from England and was now
becalmed in Bombay. Urgent messages were sent but the combination of
Indian bureaucratic obstructionism and a strike of railwaymen made
sure that it never caught up with us.

On the afternoon of Wednesday, May the 8th, we hefted our loads
once more on to a lorry, clambered on board and were off again. At the
village of Reni, fifteen miles up the valley, we halted to pick up the gang
of scruffy ruffians who were to be our porters. The next village, three
miles further on, was Lata—the end of the road.

3. The Garhwal Himalayas

Changabang stands in the central part of the Himalayas in the region
called Garhwal. Garhwal and neighbouring Kumaon came under British
control early last century. They had been native principalities but in the
opening years of the century they were invaded and conquered by
tribesmen from Nepal who then began to raid into the plains of British
India. The British fought a characteristic campaign. They were beaten in
the early encounters but gradually recovered and finally drove the
tribesmen back eastwards and took over the territories. They then con-
cluded a treaty with Nepal, establishing friendship and ensuring the
invaluable help of Gurkha mercenary soldiers in Britain's future wars.

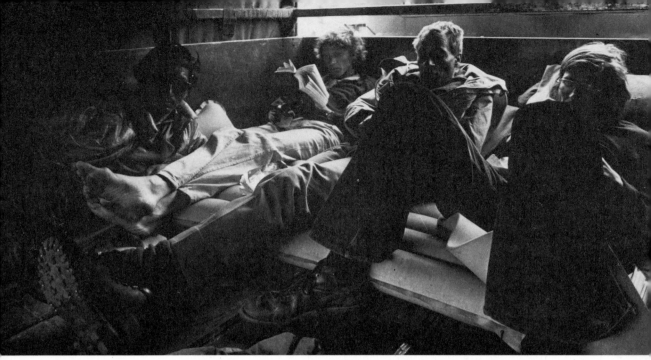

10. A mobile reading party, cocooned by the Indian army from the usual anxieties of travel.

The summit of Nanda Devi became the highest point in Britain's expanding empire and for well over a century the exploration of the area was primarily a British concern.

The first Commissioner of Garhwal and Kumaon, Mr. G. W. Traill, a remarkable man who ruled the region with total but benign authority from 1817 until 1836, made an exhaustive survey of his kingdom. In the course of his travels, without any mountaineering knowledge or experience, he crossed an 18 000 foot pass to the north-east of Nanda Devi which is still called Traill's Pass. But it was the people he was interested in, not the mountains, and he made no attempt to penetrate into the uninhabited regions of the Nanda Devi Sanctuary itself.

The first man to try to do this was Mr. W. W. Graham, a determined mountain traveller who was perhaps the first man to go to the Himalayas 'more for sport and adventures,' as he put it, 'than for the advancement of scientific knowledge.' In 1883, with two Swiss guides, he tried to find a way to the western foot of Nanda Devi by way of the great Gorge of the Rishi Ganga river. They set off up the Gorge from Reni early in July, presumably just as the monsoon was beginning, but were halted by a vertical rock wall after only four miles. So they returned to Reni and tried the approach from further north, up the Dunagiri Glacier to make an attempt on Dunagiri itself. According to Graham they got to within six hundred feet of the summit before a violent snowstorm forced them to retreat. So once again they returned to Reni and this time tried to force the Rishi Gorge by a route high up on its northern bank, the way which most subsequent visitors have taken to the Nanda Devi area. It was raining almost continuously; leeches abounded; there was much sickness, especially diarrhoea; and the porters were frightened and disaffected. Despite all this, they reached Dharansi after three days. It was snowing by then and most of the porters had left them, but Graham and his party pushed on through the forest for four more days until they reached what was probably the junction of the Rishi and the Rhamani rivers. The waters were in spate, the rest of their porters now bolted, and they had to turn back. 'We had to swag back,' Graham wrote to a friend, '60 lbs. per man, over the most awful ground. My back still aches when I think of it.'

More than twenty years passed before another serious attempt was made. In 1905 Dr. Tom Longstaff, a dedicated Alpinist, explored the country to the east of Nanda Devi, discovered and traversed what is now called the Longstaff Col and became the first mountaineer to look into the great Sanctuary. He fell in love with the area: 'I do not believe,' he wrote, 'that the scenery of Upper Garhwal can be surpassed anywhere.' Two years later he returned with a formidable team—A. L. Mumm, Charles Bruce, three Alpine guides, and several Gurkha soldiers whom Bruce had trained for hard work at high altitudes. Their chief aim was to find a route up the Rishi Gorge. They set off from Lata in early May and were turned back almost immediately by deep snow. Longstaff decided to reconnoitre the route from the north and led his party up the Bagini Glacier, over the pass between Changabang and Dunagiri and down the Rhamani Glacier. Then they turned westward and traversed high above the Rishi Gorge, more or less by the route we took to Changabang, and so back to the Dhauli valley. Longstaff's next objective was the conquest of Trisul. He marched up the Rishi Gorge for four days, forced a crossing of the river, and gained the summit on June 12th, 1907. The climb was a remarkable achievement. With the Brocherel brothers of Courmayeur and one of Bruce's Gurkhas, Kharbir, Longstaff camped at 17,500 feet, climbed nearly 6,000 feet to reach the summit at four in the afternoon, and then descended 7,000 feet before camping for the night. Trisul, 23,360 feet above sea level, was the highest point on the world's surface ever reached at that time, and remained so for the next twenty-three years.

But the Rishi Gorge was still unconquered. The last and hardest part of it, above the junction with the Rhamani, had not been penetrated and it was not until 1934 that the passage of the whole Gorge was finally accomplished. In that year two young British adventurers who had already climbed successfully together on Mount Kenya, Eric Shipton and H. W. Tilman, were inspired by what they had read and heard of

Longstaff's journeys to make the attempt themselves. In six days they covered the route Longstaff had established to the junction with the Rhamani. Above this point it is only four miles to the end of the Gorge, but the way is so broken, the river so torrential, the slopes so big and steep, the forest so thick that it took nine days of arduous and often dangerous travelling before they emerged into the inner sanctuary of Nanda Devi.

Two years later Tilman led an Anglo-American team in the first ascent of Nanda Devi. He and N. E. Odell reached the summit on August 29th, 1936. At the same period Shipton was making a thorough survey of the northern part of the Sanctuary, exploring the glaciers south of Changabang and Kalanka, peering over the big wall that drops down to the head of the Rhamani Glacier, and climbing to within one thousand feet of the summit of Dunagiri.

At last the region was explored and properly mapped, and in the years that followed some of the other main peaks were climbed: Dunagiri by a Swiss party, led by André Roch, on July 4th, 1939; Nanda Devi East on July 22nd, 1939, by a team of Polish climbers; and Nanda Ghunti by another Swiss team, again led by André Roch, on September 11th, 1947.

4. The Mountain

The nearest well-known mountains to Changabang are Nanda Devi, five miles to the south, and Kamet, on India's border with Tibet thirty miles to the north-west. Compared to giants such as these Changabang is not high and there are many hundreds of peaks in the Himalayas which outrank it in the simple statistical matter of height above sea level. But you only have to look at it, or at photographs of it, to see that there is something very special about Changabang. Nearly all the high mountains of the Himalayas are approachable from one direction at least without too much mountaineering difficulty, although icefalls and avalanches may make them highly dangerous. Changabang is uniformly unrelenting. Its granite walls sweep forbiddingly up on every side. There is no easy way and it looks to the modern climber much as the Matterhorn must have done to the early Alpinists. Every explorer who has passed that way in the last ninety years, ever since the area was first visited, has gazed up at it with wonder and awe.

W. W. Graham told the Alpine Club in London: 'Here the peaks are wild and savage in the extreme, being for the most part bare scarped rocks, too steep for snow to rest on although so far above the snow-line and remarkable for the immense number of rocky aiguilles and pinnacles which defy even the ibex and the Himalayan chamois. I do not hesitate to say that the peaks of these regions, with a few exceptions, present the most awful series of impossibilities that a climber can set eyes on.'

When Longstaff reported to the Alpine Club, he said: 'Changabang is the most superbly beautiful mountain I have ever seen; its North-West Face a sheer precipice of over 5,000 feet, being composed of such pale granite that it is at first taken for snow lying on the cliffs at an impossibly steep angle.' And many years later, in his autobiography *This My Voyage,* published in 1950, he still remembered Changabang as 'in some ways the most amazing mountain I have ever seen.'

One of Longstaff's companions was A. L. Mumm and in his book *Five Months in the Himalayas,* published in 1909, he describes Changabang as 'an immense pale brown mountain powdered with snow and with the most incredible hanging glaciers on it. With its splendid precipices rising above the col, the great eastern wall comes to an abrupt and imposing end.'

There was a gap of nearly thirty years before the area was visited again, this time by Tilman and Shipton. In 1934 Shipton scrambled up a ridge on the northern side of Nanda Devi to try to make an accurate survey of the mountains that lay to the north: 'At 4 o'clock the snow stopped falling and we erected the plane-table and waited in a bitterly cold wind for the evening clearing of the mists. At half-past five our patience was rewarded. A rift appeared to the west, and framed in it was a dome of rock and ice which could belong to only one mountain— Changabang. There was no mistaking it.' Two years later Shipton approached much nearer and walked along the foot of the mountain on its southern side: 'I sat for an hour fascinated by the gigantic white cliffs of Changabang.'

The year after that Frank Smythe, the conqueror of Kamet, looked up at Changabang from the area of the Dunagiri Col, and wondered at 'the terrible precipices of Changabang, a peak that falls from crest to glacier in a wall that might have been sliced in a single cut of a knife.'

Once again the area was left in solitude for a long time—until 1950 when W. H. Murray led the first Scottish Himalayan expedition and was deeply moved by the prospect: 'By day like a vast eye-tooth fang, both in shape and colour—for its rock was a milk-white granite—Changabang in the moonlight shone tenderly as though veiled in bridal lace; at ten miles distance seemingly as fragile as an icicle; a product of earth and sky rare and fantastic, and of liveliness unparalleled so that unaware one's pulse leapt and the heart gave thanks—that this mountain should be as it is.'

5. What's in a name?

The Garhwal Himalayas have great spiritual significance to the four hundred and forty million people of the Hindu faith. The mountains are

11. and 12. Pilgrims on the road to Badrinath.

seen as the homes of the Gods. The waters that foam down from the glaciers join together to form the holiest of rivers, 'Mother Ganges'. The temple at Badrinath, high up in the foothills, about twenty miles beyond Josimath, is one of the great places of pilgrimage, and the most familiar sight on the road up from the plains is that of the holy men, plodding along on their spindly legs, travelling hard and light, with a small brass bowl in one hand and perhaps a blanket over one shoulder. Their needs are modest but they live entirely by begging and there are so many of them in the spring and summer pilgrimage season, one or two every hundred yards or so of the way, that the local villagers and farmers must often find their faith severely tested.

The spiritual importance of the region is reflected in many of its place names. *Rishi* is the word for a wise and holy man; *Trisul* means the trident of Siva—Siva, the God of Destruction, the member of the Hindu trinity especially associated with the malignant and mysterious forces in nature; *Nanda Devi* is the Goddess Nanda, who was a bride of Siva; and *Nanda Ghunti* means the Goddess Nanda in her bridal veil. *Harunam*, the mountain alongside our Base Camp, is named after the monkey god of Hindu mythology who found a vital herb high up on the mountain and with it saved the life of another god, Rama.

In this respect, as in so many others, Changabang is exceptional. The name has, apparently, no meaning, religious or otherwise. I can find no account of its origin. It is, simply and solely, the name of the mountain of that name. And though it may give rise to some ribald punning in modern English-speaking circles, it is a name with a strong and memorable and resounding ring about it and this makes it appropriate.

4. The Approach March

1. The walk begins

Changabang is an elusive mountain. It took considerably longer to get at it than to get up it. And there were moments on the approach march when it seemed it might prove harder to find the mountain than to climb it.

From the roadside village of Lata to the site of our Base Camp was little more than twenty miles as the crow flies. But we had to travel as the man walks, and the heavily-laden man at that. And the terrain is so big and broken and remote that we must have walked at least twice that distance to complete the journey in six stages of a day's march each, some of them long and tiring days. Beyond Lata there was no village or farm or sign of human habitation, only an occasional cairn to show that local shepherds and hunters sometimes went that way. And all the way direct progress was repeatedly obstructed by big ridges, some of them thousands of feet high and all of them falling southwards, diamentrically across our path, forcing long detours and a great deal of ascent and descent. The whole journey, in fact, took us ten days because of initial trouble with the porters and shepherds.

The hillmen of Garhwal have had mixed reviews over the years from their expedition employers. W. W. Graham in the 1880s found they often 'bolted' when the going got difficult and at one point he dismissed the lot of them: 'I had to send the coolies home,' he wrote to a friend, 'as the brutes had eaten a fortnight's food in five days.' But fifty years later Eric Shipton was sufficiently impressed with his porters from Lata to tell the Royal Geographical Society: 'It is time someone undertook the task of training these people as mountaineers.' Our experience of them fell between these extremes.

They were undeniably dirty. They wore thick and ragged homespun jackets and trousers, riddled with holes and patches, and decrepit boots and shoes. They were prone to fleas and sickness, especially dysentery. They smoked whenever they could whatever they could get hold of, and spent much of the time between puffs hawking and spitting, coughing and wheezing, clearing their throats and voiding their sinuses with shameless abandon. But they were also strong and accomplished hill walkers. Each man carried a load of just over sixty pounds, strapped to his back usually by a rucksack-type harness improvised out of old rope.

They needed little personal gear—a bit of food, cigarettes and a blanket to curl up in at night. For a working day they were paid eight rupees, about forty-five pence, plus rations. It seems poor reward for work that is always arduous and sometimes dangerous, but it is the going rate in the region and attractive enough to make them leave their farming life in the valleys for a few weeks. The twenty or so men who stayed with us and ferried our supplies to Base Camp were generally cheerful, once the march was properly under way, and unfailingly helpful. And though there must have been many times when some of our things—cameras, transistor radios, tape recorders—seemed temptingly available, nothing was stolen.

Our initial plan was to employ sixty porters but two other sizable expeditions had preceded us into the area and we could only raise thirty. So the resourceful Kiran hired two hundred goats and sheep with four shepherds to herd them. Ballu later described the complications involved in using goats:

Ballu:

A goat carries approximately twenty-two pounds—depending on its size, sex, pregnancy state, disposition and status in the herd. Working out goat wages is endlessly amusing and eventually we pay for the total weight carried by the herd divided by the number of porters it would have required and add to this the food those porters would eat. Rum Doodlish! The goats are content to carry their saddle bags secured front and rear. They protest only at the time of loading and when you see how it is done, it is no surprise that they do. Of course, the saddle bag carries small items. This means breaking up loads that have been meticulously packed for the porters into a chaotic dump. And you never can tell which goat has what until you unstitch the saddle bags on reaching Base Camp and pour the contents out, rather like a Sunday bazaar. Both Tashi and DJ are incensed at seeing all their toil in packing wasted, and more so when, as menu-planners, they find they cannot get at, say, biscuits or tea leaves. Doesn't make them or the goats very popular.

Hank:

Sherpa Tashi, who had walked up the Rishi Gorge before *en route* for Nanda Devi, gleefully warned us about the first day's march: 'It's straight up,' he said, 'from seven thousand feet above sea level to twelve thousand. Steep and slippery and hard. It's a real beginning to an expedition.' He was not exaggerating, though the first part was pleasant enough—through the village of Lata, then along a wide path among terraced barley fields with wild roses and marijuana flourishing in the hedges, and into the cool conifer forest. An hour and a half or so of gradual ascent brought us to a clearing with a stream sparkling through, and it was here that we had our first trouble.

13. **The end of the road. Just below the village of Lata and above the Dhauli River,** animals and loads are sorted out for the approach march.

14. and 15. Loading up the animals.

The shepherds had gone ahead of us and halted here, unloaded their charges and turned them loose to graze. Ballu wanted to know what the idea was. The chief shepherd said the next stage was long and hard, five hours at least, so they would camp here and go on tomorrow. Since it was still only ten thirty in the morning, Ballu was not having that. A lengthy argument began.

We watched for a while, then left them to it and set off up the steep forest path, scrambling among the rocks and tree roots. It was enjoyable at first, but before long I began to feel sensations I had not experienced for four years, ever since the Annapurna South Face expedition—the blood pounding behind my ears, leg muscles protesting, gasping for breath through an ever-open mouth, a dry throat. The path was relentless and seemed to be endless. My stops became more frequent, but at least it grew cooler—I was soon to learn that this was due more to the regular afternoon incursion of bad weather than to any gain in altitude—and we emerged, at last, in the late afternoon, on to a wide grassy ridge just above the last straggly line of pines and birches and rhododendron. We soon had a wood fire blazing and Martin gathered leaves and set about brewing a welcome infusion of birch tea while we waited for the others.

This was Lata Kharak—the grazing grounds of Lata.

Most of the porters reached the camp by nightfall but not all of them and one vital load was missing—the cigarettes. This was a serious matter and the porters retired to the forest to settle down for the night with many expressions of discontent.

Immediately after breakfast the next day we noticed the porters gathered in a tight, gesticulating group on the slope below our tents. Kiran went to pacify them while Chris and Doug brought out a battery of cameras to record the happening.

The porters had a catalogue of grievances. They had spent a cold night under the trees and were not looking forward to going higher and getting colder. Their rations had been inadequate. Bereft of cigarettes, they were unable to shit satisfactorily. Furthermore, they had no guarantee of proper medical attention. It appears that the previous morning, before the approach march started, DJ had found himself confronted by a sizable sick parade of porters. He was preparing to hand out a selection of pills and potions when Tashi dissuaded him. Tashi, who had scant respect for Garhwalis, argued that they were plainly malingering, had not even begun to work, and merely wanted to stock up with medicines

16. **The porters at Lata Kharak, with not a cigarette between them.**

for possible future needs or to use for barter. He may well have been right, but it was a serious tactical error to refuse medical assistance at that stage.

The dispute continued throughout the day. Like a swarm of furious bees, the porters swirled and buzzed about, rising at times to a crescendo of indignation, then subsiding into steady rumblings. Kiran, the eternal dogsbody, represented the employers' side in the negotiations. There were moments when he disappeared from view in the crowd of porters and we only knew he was still in there pitching by the sound of his high tenor riding the storm of protest. Then he would emerge and stride across to report to Ballu who sat apart, aloof and unperturbed, the ultimate arbiter. From time to time some of the more militant porters would suddenly turn away from the discussion, shoulder their belongings and make off towards the homeward path with a purposeful air. But soon after they came edging back to rejoin the battle. The weather increased our apprehensions for once again, in the early afternoon, the sunshine turned to dank cold and cloud and large wet snowflakes began to fall.

Next morning everything was brighter. The sun shone once more. The porters—apart from the handful who had carried out their threat to go home—had spent a more comfortable night. The cigarettes had arrived. The sheep and goats were loaded early and moved off in long procession up the slopes above the camp, the tinkling of their bells giving the scene a cheerful, Alpine air. God was in his heaven and we were on our way again.

17. For their second night's stay at Lata Kharak the porters set up a tarpaulin shelter.

18, 19 and 20. Lata close-ups.

At first the way led up a gentle grassy slope, then contoured north-wards and across scattered fields of fresh snow till we gained a high pass at about thirteen thousand five hundred feet. It was a dramatic place. Ahead the land broke up into a dark jumble of steep rocky ridges. It looked as though there could be no possible way through. But the shepherds assured us there was a path, which they followed each summer to find rich pasture, though they made it clear with vigorous gestures that it was not to be taken carelessly.

The flock went first and we followed. It was exciting going, rough and stony and winding and offering, at many points, a fearful fall to anyone who missed his footing. Time and again it seemed that there could be no way round the next obstacle, but always at the crucial moment the path would veer and climb and twist and dip and somehow find a way, until at last the prospect opened out and we dropped gratefully down to the

21. The sheep and goats are coaxed towards the high pass above Lata Kharak.

broad green meadows of Dharansi, scattered with dwarf pink primulas and clumps of blue iris and graceful anemones.

We sat around an open log fire that evening to eat supper—soup, tinned mackerel and fresh vegetables and, for once, no rice, followed by pineapple slices. DJ had a slight altitude headache and Chris was constipated, but the rest of us felt fit and pleasantly tired. And the porters, packed together under a tarpaulin sheet for the night, were singing.

The next day, Sunday May the 12th, was largely devoted to losing height. After a short uphill pull to a pass marked by elaborate cairns called 'chortens', the path followed a long descending ridge to re-enter the forest, two thousand five hundred feet lower down. The descent continued through the cool shade and the sweet scent of mingled pine and thyme. In the valley bottom there were two torrential streams to cross, one of them bridged by felled tree trunks, then a brief climb to the lovely clearing called Dibrugheta.

Tilman described Dibrugheta as 'a horizontal oasis in a vertical desert'. It is an idyllic place—the perfect camping site, green and spacious and shaded, with unlimited firewood immediately to hand, unlimited fresh water tumbling nearby and the ground a level couch of soft leaf-mould, centuries deep. Ten thousand feet or so above sea level, the air is clean and invigorating. It is here that the path joins the Rishi Gorge itself, one thousand feet up on its northern bank.

That night, around a blazing fire, we got the porters to sing their

'Nanda Devi' song for us, a soulful ballad of romance in the high hills. We recorded their tuneless rendering on tape and played it back to them. Cigarettes were distributed. Then we sat round the fire for a long time, not saying much, watching the flames and blinking painfully when the smoke swirled our way, reluctant, for once, to turn in. Occasionally the trees would be sharply illumined for a moment by lightning and we heard the rumble of distant thunder. It was said to be brown bear country but if there were any about, they gave us a wide berth. The modern world and its complexities seemed very far away.

2. This camping life

'If the Nottingham lads could see me now, they wouldn't believe their eyes.'

Doug Scott was stretched out in the sun in a pair of shorts and nothing else, reading a paperback and occasionally reaching out to grab a handful of freshly-fried potato crisps. The rest of us were scattered about in similar attitudes.

Doug is used to rudimentary expeditions where there are no porters or Sherpas or kitchen boys to take the burden of the chores and the climbers have to do everything for themselves. The Himalayan expedition is, by comparison, effete and effortless, one of the last surviving outposts of the Sahib's life.

Throughout the approach march, the only thing the climber has to do is get himself and his rucksack, half the weight of the loads the porters are carrying, to the next camp site. He can make his own pace and stop for a rest whenever he feels like it. When he reaches the site a kitchen boy immediately proffers a mug of hot sweet tea. He sits on the ground to drink it and watch the Sherpas and the kitchen staff put up the tents and arrange the kitchen area and collect firewood. It becomes quite an effort, an imposition almost, to have to stir yourself and lay out your bedding for the night—a closed-cell foam mattress, built for insulation from cold rather than for comfort, and a down sleeping bag.

At night or in bad weather the only call to leave the tent is the call of nature. You take your boots off but nothing else—sometimes you put more clothes on to make sure of keeping warm—wriggle into the sleeping bag and lie, ranged the length of the tent like so many sardines, listening to music and reading and chatting. There is not much room for movement but who wants to move anyway? Every now and then a cook boy appears at the door flap, grinning happily through the falling snow, and tea and biscuits or mugs of hot soup are handed in and passed along the line.

Climbers have an enviable capacity for total inactivity. When there is nothing to be done, they do it wholeheartedly. When they are not absolutely vertical, they like to be absolutely horizontal. And they maintain their inertia, if necessary, for days on end. It is an art that has been perfected, presumably, over years of camping in places, from North Wales to Nepal, where the weather can be bad for prolonged periods.

There were times on the approach march and at Base Camp when we looked more like a reading party than an expedition. My own reading was light enough, stories by Lionel Davidson and H. R. F. Keating and Patricia Highsmith, and Ballu was immersed in the sexual and intellectual adventures of Henry Miller. The others put us to shame. Chris was lost to the world hour after hour in a thick volume by Herman Wouk. Dougal devoured Alan Bullock's biography of Hitler and Nietzsche's theories on Greek tragedy. Martin chuckled to himself, infuriatingly, over *Bleak House*. And Doug made a determined assault on the classics, *The Odyssey, The Search for the Holy Grail, The Pillow Book of Sei Shōnagon,* and James Joyce's *Ulysses*.

In music, too, the general taste was for the classics. We had tapes of Mozart, Haydn, Handel and Beethoven whose violin concerto—the Heifetz recording—was played most often. But there was Cleo Laine as well and some modern jazz and pop. Ballu preferred these.

Expedition life is strange in many ways, basic and uncomplicated and completely cut off from normal routine. On Changabang, once we had left the road, we had scarcely any contact with the world outside apart from Ujagar's transistor radio which spoke languages we did not understand. The only item of news that got to us in more than a month was that India had exploded an atom bomb. The rest was silence. Only one batch of mail reached us, weeks late, and though we wrote letters from time to time it was with the feeling, justified by the event, that we would probably get home before they did.

The pace of things is slow, the decisions that have to be made are few and simple. It is a life of contradictions. You alternate between near-euphoria and near-despair, between hard physical effort and complete idleness. The air around is pure and clean but you become grubby. Personal hygiene goes by the board when all you have to wash with is a handful of snow. There is little point in changing your clothes. The daily exercise makes you fit but the altitude often makes you feel terrible. You live communally, thrown together in an intimate group, but you spend long hours alone with your thoughts and find yourself brooding over matters like the state of your bowels or whether you are acclimatising to the altitude properly or where the hell some piece of your equipment

22. The animals rest and pay no attention to the mass of Dunagiri, 23 184 ft, behind them.

can have got to. Small things loom ridiculously large, sensations are heightened, impressions intensified.

There is much more time than usual for leisurely conversation and the talk ranges widely—from the purpose and meaning of human life and the curing of the world's ills to personal reflection and reminiscence. Something about the situation inclines men to become introspective and confessional. Much of the talk, naturally, is about the climb itself, how things are going, plans for the immediate future, the chances of success. But there is a lot of talk, too, about former climbs and climbing companions. The characters of absent friends are analysed and sometimes assassinated. One subject is conspicuous by its virtual absence. There must be more talk about sex in any lunchtime half-hour in any British pub than there was throughout the whole of the Changabang expedition.

The food was always plentiful and usually good. The Garhwal region is largely vegetarian and the shepherds refused all offers for one or two of their animals for slaughtering, so we got no fresh meat, but there was tinned meat and fish and plenty of fresh vegetables, rice and potatoes and some greens. The fruit was tinned, with one heart-warming exception—rhubarb, which we found flourishing in the damp gullies above Dibrugheta. Rhubarb became, briefly, an expedition obsession. People went on rhubarb recces, and everyone who moved around in the rhubarb-growing regions was expected to bring some back. We extolled its properties as 'nature's pullthrough' and whiled away the hours of idleness by devising increasingly unlikely ways of serving it—rhubarb *flambée,* rhubarb and chips, rhubarb *sur le plât* Rishi Gorge, rhubarb soup. It led in the end to trouble in the kitchen and DJ, who was our catering officer as well as the doctor, came to me anxiously one morning to say that the head cook, Sherpa Norbu, had refused to make rhubarb soup and doubted if it was possible. I had to admit that Norbu was right.

At six each morning, with first light, a kitchen boy would appear to hand mugs of tea into the Sahibs' tent. Breakfast, an hour or two later, consisted of porridge or cornflakes with hot milk and sugar, an omelette, then chapattis and either jam or honey. Sometimes there would be coffee, usually tea. On days when we were on the move we did not bother with lunch. Each man would carry what he wanted, a bar of chocolate, perhaps a tin of sardines, and a couple of small tins of fruit juice, grapefruit or mango. Supper was the day's main meal—a mug of soup, a plate of meat with either rice or potatoes and some other vegetable, and finally jelly or tinned fruit, sometimes both. Some evenings we would pass the whisky bottle round or open a few cans of Indian beer.

The nights were long. After supper we would try to read for a while by the light of candles or pocket torches, but the eyes soon grow tired of that. There was nothing else for it, about nine o'clock, but to try to get to sleep. It was not always easy. Ujagar's transistor radio might be going, full blast, in a neighbouring tent. You could listen to the night chorus of coughs and try to guess who they came from. Chris and I were both accused of snoring. But the worst thing of all sprang from the noxious turmoil which a diet of rice and rich spices induced in the guts of Martin and Dougal. I remember, with painful clarity, one particular night when I seriously considered moving my bed out into the snow to escape the fumes: It seemed such a dreadful way to go—to be asphyxiated by farts at ten thousand feet above sea level, surrounded by the cleanest air in the world.

3. Norbu—a link with the past

It soon became obvious that the other Sherpas had enormous respect for Norbu, our sixty-two-year-old head cook. Sensible and hungry people will always strike up a good relationship with the cook. With Norbu it came easily, both to the Sherpas and to us. He had seen it all before. Expedition life for him began in the early 1930s when he went as a kitchen boy on Ruttledge's Everest expedition—in the days when Everest visitors had to make the long march across the high Tibetan plateau to the northern side of the mountain. He had carried the young Norman Dyhrenfurth on his shoulders when he was just a baby, trekking round Kangchenjunga with his father, G. O. Dyhrenfurth. He'd since been on Japanese, French and American expeditions as well as several British ventures—all over the Himalayas.

Norbu was born at Thame in Khumbu, the Sherpa people's home area, but later moved down to the Sherpa colony at Darjeeling, where he lives with his wife and family on a small hill-farm. His daughter works at an embassy in Kathmandu. One of his sons was killed in a climbing accident during a Japanese expedition in Nepal. But despite this, and his frequent long absences from home, Norbu is only saddened by the prospect of retirement from expedition life. While he may carry a smaller sack than he once did, he can still conjure up a variety of good tacks from a few basic ingredients, often in appalling conditions. We never saw him, or any other Sherpa for that matter, lose his temper. They have a ready sense of humour that smoothes out local difficulties such as spluttering kerosene stoves and rain-soaked branches that refuse to light.

It was while sheltering from the rain in his kitchen tent, along with Tashi and some porters, that I tried to find out what Norbu thought of us as compared to his pre-war employers.

Of all his many experiences, Norbu remembers none so vividly as those with H. W. Tilman. According to Norbu, Tilman was always away first in the morning, carrying a load in excess of the standard Sherpa load. He always arrived first at the day's destination—sometimes he'd run along parts of the route. He would have tea brewing by the time the rest of them caught up with him, and then he'd praise those who'd made good time and yell and scream at those he thought had been lazy or lacking in some way. On at least one rest day he made all his Sherpas a cake—Tashi, who was translating all this for me, was made to repeat this fact several times. He was always the first to cross turbulent streams, pass hard rocky sections, and shoulder awkward loads. He was obviously a born leader and Norbu, at any rate, was still very impressed.

What, I asked, does old Norbu think of us moderns? There was no hesitation. We were softies—wrapped up in the finest down that money could buy, as far a cry from heavy tweeds as our light-weight double boots are from the tattered nailed boots that Tilman and Shipton wore when they left Nanda Devi in 1934.

And what of our superb kitchen equipment and the wide variety of food to titillate our genteel palates? Compare it with Shipton's victualling for their first visit to Nanda Devi: 'Our food was very simple. It consisted mainly of flour, rice and ghee (clarified butter) which we bought as we went along. We had brought various luxuries to supplement these: sugar, tea, lentils, a number of 10 lbs. Cheddar cheeses sewn up in cloth, and some tins of pemmican.' Salts and spices were the only additions. Tilman was 'indifferent to what we took so long as it was food and not chemicals and gave value for weight . . . in my opinion all tinned foods tasted the same.' Tilman recognised that it was difficult to satisfy everyone so it was 'all the more important, therefore, to get this job (of provisioning) done before any other members of the party arrived further to darken counsel by urging the claims of their pet foods.'

These two hard men lived off the land whenever possible. While they were crossing an unknown pass in the Badrinath region their staple diet, Shipton wrote, 'was bamboo shoots . . . except where hungry bears had forestalled us, it was fairly easy to collect a potful of the little green cylinders which, boiled, constituted our evening meal.' Their attitudes and styles have entered the folk-lore of mountain exploration—their days of total silence because there was nothing worth saying that had not been said before, the schism between them over whether to take one shirt or two on a three-month journey.

It is tempting to run away with the romantic notion that the pre-war men were more 'pushy' and hardy than today's explorers. Perhaps it is not so. Norbu himself was full of admiration for our effort on Changa-

23. Sherpa Norbu. Cook and veteran of many expeditions.

bang, where, when it came to the crunch, we disappeared for five days carrying all our own equipment and food up very hard and steep terrain—harder, perhaps, than pre-war expeditions would tackle.

Yet in reality it is only a continuing process. We are able to go for steeper objectives because our equipment is better and lighter—a three-man nylon tent, now, weighs 8 lbs. and our sleeping bags only 3 lbs. We have efficient gas stoves and freeze-dried foods that weigh a fraction of pre-war rations. And we have prior knowledge of the area—Shipton's accurate maps and measurements and even photographs. We also have more understanding of the debilitating effects of altitude and dehydration. And all this gives us enormous confidence. Then there's another factor, perhaps the most important, that we have seen others reach comparable standards elsewhere. They have broken through psychological barriers. We should be able to repeat what they did and then, all things being equal, push on further.

4. The Big Wall

The stage after Dibrugheta was short, easy and delightful—a contouring walk high up on the northern side of the Rishi Gorge across the slopes of cotoneaster and prostrate juniper, with commanding views all the way of the dark chasm of the Gorge and the great snow slopes above and beyond it, culminating in the icy summit of Nanda Devi East. Three hours of exhilarating walking brought us to the camp site of Deodi, a small clearing among birch trees.

It was here that we said goodbye to the sheep and goats. For towering above Deodi and right across our path stood a monstrous cliff, dark and steep and 1,500-feet high. The shepherds were not going to risk their animals on it and it was hard to blame them. I was reluctant to risk it myself.

We spent several days at Deodi, waiting for all the loads to catch up with us, waiting for Chris and Dougal to find a site for Base Camp, and trying to find a way round what we came to call the Big Wall.

The more I looked at it, the less I liked it. From the camp, almost directly underneath the Wall and face on, it seemed nearly vertical. Its rock looked unreliable, its scattered vegetation loose and slimy. There were clearly many places where a slip would mean plunging hundreds of feet to the boulder-strewn gully at its foot. H. W. Tilman, when he came across the Wall in the 1930s, had viewed it with repugnance: 'I was never fond of it,' he wrote, 'disliked it especially coming down, and

24. The Rishi Gorge.

dreaded it when wet.' To my wary eyes, it seemed to be wet most of the time.

During our first two days at Deodi a couple of parties ventured up it to investigate the ground beyond—Chris and Doug, Dougal and Ballu, together with the most sure-footed of our porters, Kishen Singh. I watched the tiny figures moving carefully about high above and hoped we would find a safer alternative. The reports they brought back were not reassuring. 'It's a fabulous bloody cliff,' Chris said with his usual enthusiasm, 'quite hard in places and really dodgy. I don't feel happy about asking the porters to go that way. There wouldn't be much chance for anyone who came off.'

On the third day Chris and Dougal set off up the Wall to establish the next camp and Ballu went along with a couple of kitchen boys to help carry the loads. We had a lazy day, sun-bathed through the morning, and when the clouds rolled up the valley in the early afternoon to turn summer into winter crept into the tent to listen to Beethoven's Seventh Symphony and some of Doug's more disreputable reminiscences. The storm went on all afternoon and when it finally cleared, at six in the evening, the Wall was plastered with fresh snow. Ballu and the kitchen boys were due to come back for the night but when darkness fell and they had not returned we assumed, hopefully, that they had decided to stay higher up until tomorrow.

Suddenly, just when it had got really dark, we heard shouts from high up on the Wall. Our hearts sank. They were up there, tired from their long day, in darkness, on a dangerous cliff that was now more dangerous than ever. 'Jesus Christ!' said Martin, as we pulled on our boots and down jackets, 'this is just what we bloody needed!'

It was a brilliant, clear night, with no moon but many glittering stars and the whole area bathed in dim snow-light. Tashi joined us, desperately anxious, as Doug and Martin sorted out a five hundred foot rope and some pitons. Our torches were running low and cast only the faintest beams.

We moved off towards the Wall, clutching at the bushes, staggering and slithering about in the snow to a vantage point near the bottom. Doug was muttering angrily. 'It's bloody crazy. The Wall's bad enough in daylight, in good conditions. They must be mad to have got on to it now.'

We shouted up and got some answering yells. Doug raised his voice to its full strength and called: 'Ballu! You must bivouac! It's too dangerous to move about up there now. Stay where you are and bivouac. We'll get you down at first light.' There were more answering shouts but we could make nothing out. Then silence. We waited a few minutes, then tried again. There was no reply. They must have taken our advice, we thought, and gone back over the summit ridge to shelter for the night. Relieved, we stumbled back to the camp to warm ourselves at the kitchen fire.

But we had only been there a minute or so when we heard Ballu's voice, loud and calm and clear: 'We are half-way down the Wall already. We cannot go back. We will be all right. Can you come to meet us with lights? We must come down.'

Kishen Singh was the first to move. He grabbed the kitchen lantern, by far the best light we had, and made off into the darkness. By the time we had collected the rope and the other gear and scrambled up to the base of the Wall by the feeble light of our two torches, he was well on his way. We stopped on a ledge and watched the lantern light bobbing about above us and to the right, moving continuously and casting huge black shadows. There was no point in us all going on and much sense in not.

We waited, feeling miserable and inadequate and praying that we would not hear the expected cry and the thud of a body on the rocks below.

'It's all wrong,' said Martin. 'Exactly what shouldn't happen. Galloping off to the rescue like some *Boy's Own Paper* bloody hero without any thought at all.'

Doug was equally furious: 'It's got nothing to do with mountaineering as we know it. I was afraid something like this would happen. What's it going to be like if they're like this on Changabang? There'll be bad weather and big winds and they'll be charging about in all directions.'

We waited for twenty minutes. Kishen Singh's lantern had disappeared from direct view but we could see its light palely reflected on the crag and it was still moving.

There was nothing we could do so we went back to the kitchen fire. Tashi was there and very distressed. 'It's not right, Sahib. A crazy business. Accidents always happen in descending. It is too dangerous. The conditions are not fit.'

But half an hour later, to our immense relief, we heard people coming down the final path and Ballu's unmistakable voice, as strong and confident as ever.

'I'm awfully sorry to have disturbed your evening in this way, gentlemen,' he said, making for the fire. 'It was very silly of us. I can't apologise enough. God, my feet are frozen!'

As we sat him down by the fire and got his boots and socks off and plunged his feet into a basin of hot water, and the two kitchen boys who had been with him were attended to as well, we got the full story. After a long march they had found a good site for Base Camp, and helped Chris and Dougal to set up their tent. It was four o'clock before they

set off back and they walked immediately into a snow-storm. They had a nightmare journey over very rough ground. They missed the path and lost each other at times. Ballu had a slight fall and cut his head. He and one of the kitchen boys began to lose feeling in their feet. He had decided not to bivouac because he was afraid a night out would mean serious frost-bite and an end to his chances of climbing the mountain.

Kishen Singh, known to us as 'Kitchen Sink', was the hero of the hour. He was an unlikely figure for a hero—scruffy and dirty, a compulsive cadger of cigarettes, racked with dysentery, with a permanent hang-dog air about him, but he was a superb natural crag-man. He wore a pair of ancient rubber-soled shoes and carried a long stick and with these he was enviably able to move with speed and apparent ease over the most difficult ground, usually keeping one hand in the pocket of his tattered trousers.

We drank his health in brandy and he forced a wan smile.

Ballu's feet were recovering in the hot water, but DJ was still solicitous.

'May I suggest, sir,' he said, 'that you have a hot water bottle in your sleeping bag tonight?'

'I'd rather have a hot woman,' Ballu replied.

'I can prescribe that, sir, but I cannot provide it,' said the doctor.

The usual platitudes were exchanged and someone said, 'All's well that ends well.' I wondered if it were. After all, it had not ended yet. The expedition had hardly begun and the serious climbing lay ahead. Doug and Martin were plainly, understandably, apprehensive. If this sort of thing could happen here, where the going was comparatively straight-forward, what was it going to be like on the climb itself? What kind of difficulties and dangers might arise from the sheer adventurousness of the Indians? No-one doubted their courage but there were grounds for concern about their caution and common sense.

Ballu said nothing but he must have been wondering too. At the first crisis of the expedition, he had been rescued, not by his British climbing comrades of high reputation but by an unknown, middle-aged Garhwali farmer. But his subsequent account of the incident had no hint of rancour:

Ballu:

We reached the crest of the Big Wall about 9 p.m. Camp lights twinkle far below. The faint track we had come up is invisible under the snow. This is dodgy! Unless we follow the track we are quite likely to spend the night out on the face. Surely and safely we lose height. Only 1000 feet more to go. Up this little incline and there should be the cairn I made in the morning. No cairn here. Try another rise. Must find the cairn for near.

25. Kishen Singh, porter, natural hill-man and hero of the Big Wall episode. We sometimes wondered if he were the oriental reincarnation of Haskett Smith, 'the father of rock climbing'.

it is the only safe chute to clamber down. We retrace our steps and, now thoroughly cold, try again. No luck. We yell across to the camp and help is on its way. Doug and Martin prepare to give us a fixed rope. We are now less than 500 feet above the camp. Porter Kishen Singh romps up with a pressure lamp and guides us down to camp—thoroughly wet and wiser.

It snowed again, heavily, during the night.

5. A question of leadership

The decision that Chris and Dougal should move ahead of the rest of us to find a suitable site for Base Camp and, incidentally, get the first look at Changabang, was made on the second day of our stay at Deodi, and the way in which it was made led to the first serious clash of the expedition. It raised the whole prickly question of expedition leadership: How should the major decisions be made? In democratic conclave, by general discussion leading to consensus agreement or some sort of vote? Or by leaving it to chance, drawing lots or tossing up for the more glamorous assignments? Or by the arbitrary orders of the acknowledged leader? Or by some compromise mixture of these methods? It is important to get it right. Mountaineers are individualistic and outspoken and sensitive to the possibility that others might steal all the interesting work and hog the subsequent limelight. And in the Himalayas the stakes are high. There is considerable glory to be gained from a successful ascent, while the price of bad decisions or fierce divisions among the team can be the failure of the expedition and even the deaths of climbers.

On the morning of the second day at Deodi the five British team members were sharing a large tent and as soon as the early morning mug of tea had been handed in to us, Chris launched a discussion about our immediate plans.

First of all there was the problem of the loads. Supplies and porters were now strung out between Deodi and Lata Kharak where Kiran and Ujagar were whipping in the stragglers. It was agreed that Tashi should be asked to go back part of the way to help them and try to get everyone to Deodi by the following evening.

Then there was the Big Wall. No-one was happy about it as a porter route. We were not sure that all the porters would be willing to attempt it and certain that if the attempt were made and one of them fell the others would abandon the expedition altogether. There was general agreement that we should try to find a less hazardous alternative. Martin and Doug and I 'said we would explore the gully that led upwards, along the foot of the Wall, to see if there was a way over the top. Chris and Dougal and Ballu would drop down towards the Rishi to try to find a low-level route.

There was one more point. 'Tomorrow,' Chris said, 'I think we should push a small, two-man party out to find a place for our Base Camp and stay there to recce the route further on and have a look at the mountain.' We had not yet seen Changabang. We all agreed.

'Well I think I ought to go ahead,' said Chris, 'and I'd like to take Dougal with me. Is that O.K.?' There was a pause, no-one objected and Chris went off to discuss the plans with Ballu.

It seemed to go off quite amicably and democratically, but at the end of the day's exploration, which had been fruitless, I arrived back in camp a few minutes behind Doug and Martin to find them in heated dispute with Chris.

Doug had started it. He has an instinctive aversion to authority and strong views on expedition leadership. When he goes to Baffin Island or elsewhere with his Nottingham mates, there is, it seems, no leader. They all muck in and get on with it and when there are decisions to make they talk and wrangle until an agreed view-point emerges. In this way, Doug believes, you get the best out of everybody with the best possible spirit prevailing. It sounds ideal and it works well, apparently, when all the climbers are old friends and know each other's special abilities and limitations. Whether such a system would work on a big Himalayan climb, with climbers who do not know each other so well and of mixed nationalities, is more questionable.

At all events, Doug had not liked the way he had been presented that morning with the decision that Chris and Dougal would make the Base Camp recce. He felt that Chris had pulled a fast one. He had been brooding on it all day and now he was having it out. Martin also rather resented the way they had been presented with a virtual *fait accompli,* though he did not feel as strongly about it as Doug.

When the expedition was over I asked the chief protagonists, Chris and Doug, to set down their thoughts.

Chris:

I have always been quite sensitive to atmosphere, but I did not need to be very sensitive to realise that the team was anything but happy when I announced that Dougal and I would go on the recce. I was not entirely happy myself. I had undoubtedly been clumsy in putting my plan across. When I asked for comments there was no dissent, but there was an intangible atmosphere of disapproval.

Up to this point in the expedition there had been no decision problems for the British climbers. Responsibility for getting us to the foot of Changabang had fallen largely on Ballu and the Indian climbers. But now we had reached a point where we could play a more active part. I felt that I should go forward on the recce because, as co-leader of the trip, I would have to take responsibility once we got back to civilisation if anything had gone badly wrong. And I had asked Dougal to come along with me because I had a special respect for his mountain judgement—a respect that Martin and Doug, who had not climbed with him so much, could not be expected to share.

The immediate problem that day, though, was to find a good safe route round the steep wall opposite our camp site. The most promising way seemed to be round the bottom of the wall where a series of grass-covered ledges led tantalisingly round the nose of the ridge. Dougal, Ballu and I investigated this route.

Tensions evaporated as we scrambled down a juniper-covered spur into the bottom of the gully. Then we tried to find the best way round. Ballu fancied a line of ridges just above the bottom of the gully and quickly disappeared among the maze of rocks above us. Dougal and I picked our way among the grassy ledges lower down till we reached a point where we could see up the other side. We waited for Ballu, but he had vanished. Dougal, always economic of effort, decided to return to camp, but I was anxious to get up the other side to make sure the whole route was feasible.

The juniper was as dense and almost as impenetrable as a barbed wire entanglement. There was a buzz of flies in the air, which was heavy with the smells of leaf-mould and vegetation. I felt lethargic yet happy—passed a little hollow that was full of animal droppings, presumably mountain goat—wondered what I should do if I met a bear face to face—felt as if I were the first man ever to penetrate the Rishi Gorge—then had the illusion shattered when I stumbled upon an empty cartridge case, the relic of a local hunter.

I plodded up the hillside towards a scar in the ridge far above.

I saw Ballu when I was about half way up. He had found another way round the Big Wall. We shouted to each other and I made my way across to him to find that he'd had an epic ascent, climbing several stretches of rock that he would not have liked to have had to reverse.

We sat in the sun and discussed the plan. Ballu was another who was put out by my proposal to push forward with Dougal. Understandably, he was worried about the way the Indian climbers were now strung out behind us, trying to hurry our supplies along. If the British climbers now surged out in front, it would look as if they were determined to grab all the glory.

26. *Top:* Looking eastwards along the Rishi Gorge with the main summit of Nanda Devi, 25 645 ft, dominating the distance. Our approach march route crossed the ridge on the left, then swung northwards. We had still not, at this stage, seen Changabang.

27. *Below:* Throughout the approach march, the southern prospect, across the Rishi Gorge, afforded a marvellous and constantly-changing panorama.

I explained my thinking to Ballu. He could not possibly be spared from Deodi until we'd managed to ferry all our supplies up to the Base Camp site. He and the other Indians were the only ones who could properly communicate with the porters. The British team, on the other hand, were fairly superfluous until we reached Base Camp. They would be best employed pushing the route out as quickly as possible.

Ballu accepted the force of the reasoning, our differences were settled, and we set off down the Wall. We soon lost the tenuous path and began zig-zagging back and forth across the net-work of grassy ledges, but even so we reached Deodi well ahead of the other party which had been looking for a route higher up.

Martin was the first to arrive and, to our surprise, he appeared from below rather than above the camp. He was slightly disgruntled. They had missed the route down the Big Wall and, as a result, had had to drop all the way down to the foot of the Gorge, rounding the spur at a point even lower than the route we had taken.

Doug, who had been taking photographs, arrived—with Hank close behind him—half an hour later. He was obviously still upset and I decided to try to clear the air.

'What's the trouble, Doug? Do you mind Dougal and me going out on the recce?'

'It's not that I mind you going. It's the way you did it.' And he launched into a positive onslaught.

I was appalled by his vehemence but, at the same time, I could see his point. I could certainly appreciate his suggestion that we should have tossed up or drawn straws to decide who should make the recce. It had simply never occurred to me when I made the decision. I have never believed in leaving the outcome of any activity to chance—have always tried to weigh up the plans and the suitability of the team-members to carry them out. This kind of careful calculation is very necessary on big expeditions like Everest and Annapurna. But here I could see Doug's point of view. As far as experience and judgement went the four of us were virtually equals. True, I had been climbing longer than the others— I was eight years older than them—but after a time you reach a level of saturation and I think all of us had reached it. I was happy to concede that it would have been better, in this case, to have tossed up for it and even offered to do so now, but Doug, having made his point, was now prepared to accept the *fait accompli*.

Doug:

What Martin and I found so annoying was that there was no suggestion or discussion—simply the bald statement—and, more to the point, I suppose, why those two? All five of us sat there side by side in the tent, conscious of a sustained silence. I skipped through half a dozen pages of

Shónagon's Pillow Book without reading a word, and Martin hardly did justice to *Bleak House*.

That same night, on returning to camp, I went for Chris. 'Chris,' I said, 'about you and Dougal going off to Base Camp for three days. You can't make arbitrary decisions like that. We'd never do it on our Nottingham trips. Why on Baffin Island . . .' and so on, eulogising the virtues of a somewhat different kind of expedition. 'And, anyway, don't you think Martin and I have had just as much route-finding experience over the years as you two? You shouldn't have brought us if you think we're not up to it. You'll end up surrounding yourself with a gang of mindless yes-men if we don't speak up about this one.'

It all came out in a prickly rush, some truth, some idealism, all built up and overstated, causing Martin to temporise, Hank to harmonise and giving Dougal his turn to skip a few pages of his book.

'Well, I knew something was wrong as soon as I made the decision, but why have you taken so long to bring it up?' asked Chris.

'Perhaps I waited too long, but I wanted to stop seething first.'

'No doubt it's the tank commander still in me,' Chris continued—and some time later ' . . . maybe I'm finding it difficult to adjust after Everest but really someone has to be leader especially when we are dealing with the Indian contingent.'

We conceded that might be necessary and that we could not have found a better formula than he had in the politicking, but now on the mountain we had to have a change of heart. After more thought, Chris typically recanted and apologised and offered to pull straws. We did not need to by then but we all agreed it would be better next time, if only to keep me from blowing a gasket.

Chris:

Our feelings at the time were intense. The matter was blown up out of all proportion. But expeditions are like that. You are in a tiny enclosed world where the ascent of a peak becomes all-important. In this particular storm in a teacup, Martin and Dougal remained unaffected— Martin because he's more easy-going, Dougal because he was sitting pretty anyway, going on the recce, but also because he has a deep self-control and self-confidence which enable him to sit out any row or conflict of interest quietly. These qualities enabled him to emerge from the ill-fated International Everest Expedition with neither enemies nor criticism.

Doug and I rubbed each other up the wrong way more than once on the expedition. The chief reason, I suspect, is that we are similar in character in some ways, both a bit obsessive, with a tendency to jump to conclusions. Yet we each, I think, valued our relationship sufficiently and had enough mutual respect to heal quickly any breach that our hot words might have made.

Doug:

Chris does not find it easy to share the decision-making, but he is adaptable to changing circumstances. In the traditional role of leader it is hard to fault him. He plays the game naturally, finding it all very satisfying while the machinery he has created moves along without incident. And when problems arise he is ready to shoulder all the blame —just as he is ready to accept the media acclaim when all goes well. For example, after his Everest expedition in 1972, when Tony Tigh was killed in the icefall and the Nepalese authorities pointed out that Tony had had no permit to climb and Chris had no right to allow him past Base Camp, Chris accepted total responsibility. It never occurred to him to say that all the other members of the team had agreed that Tony should go on the mountain. Chris bears the brunt of a lot of malicious and envious talk, and however misinformed it is, he accepts it—indeed, he expects it—and takes it in his stride.

Our crossing of swords at Deodi cleared the air and after it our relationship grew stronger daily—although that may have had much to do with our being in the heart of some of the most beautiful country we had ever seen.

Hank:

It was, as Chris says, a storm in a teacup. It did not matter greatly who went and found a site for Base Camp and got the first look at the mountain. I was a bit shocked at the time that so petty an issue could cause such intensity of feeling among grown men. It seemed to me that the people with the real grounds for grievance were the Indian climbers, who had done all the work so far and were constantly being left in the rear. This was sensible because the Indians could speak the language of the porters and we could not, but even so it is hard to imagine a group of British climbers buckling down to these inglorious chores while their fellow climbers, of another nationality, pushed ahead towards the climbing. If the roles had been reversed there would certainly have been lots of grumbling and probably several outbursts of anger.

But the incident served some good purpose. Doug made his point and it was one of principle—that on a climb like this decision-making could and should be a communal activity—and there was no trouble over this for the rest of the expedition. If it had to happen, it was good that it should happen early, before the climbers were among serious difficulties and dangers.

5. Base Camp

1. Base Camp recce

Chris:

On May the 15th Dougal and I set out to find a site for our Base Camp, with the ever-loyal Ballu and two kitchen boys.

It was another grim, lowering day with a scud of grey cloud moving above the Gorge. We were all heavily-laden. Dougal and I were carrying our personal kit and some communal items as well—food and climbing gear.

It was three in the afternoon before we reached the shoulder that barred our way into the Rhamani Gorge. By this time the cloud had crept down the hillside above us and the occasional snowflake was gusting in the wind. I was tired, felt the altitude, grew convinced that mine was the heaviest pack of all—which was probably true as I had my entire camera system with me—was feeling every one of my thirty-nine years. I had dragged behind the others, pushing myself through the skeletal arms of burnt-out juniper just fast enough to keep the two kitchen boys in sight. Every few hundred yards I had to sit down, praying the others would find a camp site soon. At last they did—a little fold in the hillside on the edge of a moraine and above a glacier stream. There was level space for a few tents and some boulders nearby to shelter our stores.

Dougal and I were fortunate. All we had to do was pitch our tent and settle down. Ballu and the two boys had to walk all the way back to Deodi. And it was snowing hard by now with big, heavy, wet flakes. We had no primus stove and it felt rather like a reversion to childhood to be making an open fire with the juniper wood we had collected on the way up.

We were now on our own. It is one of the most satisfying moments on any expedition—to be out in front, just the two of you, with unknown ground ahead. The clouds had rolled away. We stood in the snow waiting for the water to boil, wondering how Ballu and the boys were getting on, watching the setting sun turn the breast-like summit of Trisul into a voluptuous gold.

Dougal and I have climbed together a good deal over the past eight years and I have always found him an easy companion. We do not say much to each other, spend most of the time reading, yet we have very similar views about climbing tactics and strategy. In some ways there is a strong element of the *prima donna* in Dougal's make-up but he avoids odium by his very quietness. He knows exactly what he wants to do. He combines determination and fitness to an exceptional degree and this is linked with great self-discipline, so that he can sit out bad conditions or other delays with calm, knowing that things will sort themselves out.

It was a long time before I dropped off to sleep that night. I was too excited about getting our first view of Changabang the next day.

We woke to the patter of snow on the tent roof. It was bitterly cold and miserable outside so we stayed in our sleeping bags. There was no point in going up the hill if we couldn't see anything. But about 8.30 in the morning the weather began to clear so we set about our boy scout fire-making routine again, though we cheated this time and added a liberal dose of paraffin to help the fire along.

It was eleven o'clock before we set off. We crossed the glacier stream, then followed a long curving moraine ridge with the dark mass of Rishikot looming on our right. We picked our way up the scree slopes, moving from one ridge to the next, gradually gaining height. As usual, Dougal shot ahead, and I resigned myself to a slow solitary plod. I heard a shout from above. Dougal was silhouetted on the crest of the ridge.

'I can see Changabang,' he shouted.

Another few minutes and so could I. Clouds were already playing about the mountain's summit and its base was hidden behind the moraine ridge ahead of us. But it was everything our explorer-predecessors had described—a stately cathedral of grey granite, every crack and cranny traced in ice, beautiful to behold but not to climb. And then, as we gazed, the clouds rolled in, hiding our objective from us.

We picked our way back to the tent through driving snow-flakes, well content just to have seen Changabang.

2. Deciding the route

In the next day or two we all took loads to Chris and Dougal and got our first view of Changabang. Ballu wrote: 'Hank and I take another ferry. . . . It is a clear day. Another rise and look at that mountain. It looks impregnable, its virginal arrogance intimidating; a mountain out of the imagination of an artist. Hank and the porters are some way behind. I lean against a boulder and look at Changabang. Look long and deep, like Longstaff when he wrote of it: 'The most superbly beautiful mountain I have ever seen.' The mountain hasn't a wrinkle or a scar; vestal and young.'

The site Chris and Dougal now occupied would only serve as a temporary base camp. The next two objectives were clear: to establish Base Camp proper higher up and nearer to Changabang; then to study the mountain and decide which route to attempt.

On May the 17th Doug and Martin and Tashi, with two kitchen boys and two porters, joined Chris and Dougal at temporary base.

Chris:

The morning of the 18th dawned clear—the first fine morning for more than a week. But it was 7.30 before the sun crept over the ridge of Rishikot and until then it was cold enough to inhibit any desire to leave the sleeping bag.

Dougal and I got away by 8.30, with Tashi close behind, and an hour and a half later Changabang was in view. As we pressed on beyond our high point of two days before, the landscape opened out. We could see the wide basin at the head of the Rhamani Glacier, to the right a desolation of piled boulders reaching towards the steep snow-plastered wall of Rishikot, while to the left easy-angled slopes led up to Harunam, a 21,000 foot snow peak. Changabang stood proud and dominant above the Glacier.

As we plodded on up the moraine the sheer scale of the place and the effects of altitude even as low as this, about 15,000 feet, were brought home to me. It took two more hours to reach the crest of a broad ridge of boulders that had been swept down from the flanks of Dunagiri to the east. We still could not see the entire base of Changabang, but Dougal was already doubtful about our chances of climbing the West Ridge, the route I had fancied from examining photographs back in England. And the South Ridge, which faced us, we knew to be very difficult—a complex knife-edge of granite gendarmes. The entire peak was coated in fresh snow, not only every ledge and crack but even the steep slabs on its flanks.

'I think we'd be much better off trying to get over the Shipton Col on to the Changabang Glacier and climb it from the back,' Dougal suggested. 'At least we'd be more certain of getting up that way.'

I temporised. I still wanted to see the whole peak.

And the important, immediate thing was to get a proper Base Camp established, higher up than the spot where our tents were. The wide basin at the foot of the Rhamani Glacier seemed ideal, a grassy area not far from running water and within reasonable reach of firewood. Then we could set up a camp at the head of the Glacier, just below the peak, which would be our advanced base.

On the 19th we ferried loads up to the Base Camp site, planning to move in next day.

It was a relief when Ujagar Singh and Kiran turned up that evening. I had been worried at the way all the British members were out in front, getting acclimatised to the altitude, while the Indians coped with the porters and all our supply problems in the rear. The only Indian climber to join us so far, Tashi, was suffering from a severe attack of piles. Now, though, Ujagar and Kiran could start acclimatising, while Ballu remained at Deodi to make sure supplies flowed up to Base Camp.

Hank:

The vital decision about the route to take up Changabang was made on May the 21st. Here are two accounts of that day, first from Chris, then Martin.

Chris:

From my diary: May 21st. Base Camp, but at the moment hardly a base camp at all—just four little two-man tents crouched on the grass in a flat hollow between the moraine ridge that borders the Glacier and the slopes that lead up to Harunam. Tashi is complaining of bad piles and so will rest today. Doug, Martin, Dougal and I will go up for a closer look at Changabang to decide on a route. Kiran and Ujagar are sorting out the problems of ferrying our gear up to Base Camp with the few porters who have stayed with us. In this respect my co-leader, Ballu, has done a magnificent job. He's stayed at the back almost all the way on the approach march, cajoling and at times bullying our porters to keep them going . . . .

The sun crept over the Changabang ridge at 6.30. We set out at about seven when the air was still crisp with cold, but it was eleven before we reached the upper part of the Rhamani Glacier and by then the sun was hammering down from directly above us, turning the Glacier into a huge reflector. The floor of the Glacier is covered with boulders and we pick our way along snow-filled troughs between the ridges, the snow getting softer in the heat of the day.

At last I catch up with the others, sitting on a boulder immediately opposite Changabang. We're excited yet at the same time subdued—faced at last with our objective, the reality of its difficulties are altogether too obvious. It's a monolithic, tapered tower of grey granite, plastered with fresh snow, every crack veined in ice. The right-hand skyline which forms the South Ridge is deceptive for we're looking straight on to it—it looks vertical but in fact it's a tortuous knife-edged ridge bristling with rock towers that drop down to the retaining wall of the Rhamani Glacier. The left-hand skyline, the West Ridge, is steep ice-plastered slabs that sweep up to a sheer wall capped with a huge overhang.

'That left-hand route's out of the question,' said Dougal. 'Even the South Ridge will be bloody difficult in these conditions.'

I know what he means. In the last ten days a regular weather pattern has emerged of sunny mornings when we're lucky but with clouds rolling in around eleven and snow every afternoon and evening. This means we could only expect a few hours of actual climbing each day—you need fine weather for high-standard rock climbing at this altitude.

1

2

1. The camp at the head of the Changabang Glacier commanded a view of the massive North Face of Nanda Devi and its twin summits.

2. The final stages of the climb. Half way up the East Ridge, the last man on the leading rope moves carefully upward.

Over: The four British climbers—Chris, Doug, Dougal and Martin—discuss the key problem of which route they should attempt on Changabang. The West Ridge forms the left-hand skyline. The South Ridge falls toward the camera. The only possible alternative is just out of sight round the right-hand corner, rising from the col between Changabang and the mountain on the right, Kalanka.

Over: On the morning of 4th June the summit team were approaching the last great obstacle, the East Ridge.

28. The south side of Changabang, seen from a vantage point above our Base Camp. Tom Longstaff called it 'the most superbly beautiful mountain I have ever seen'. The West Ridge, rising from the left, was the route originally intended. The South Ridge falls towards the camera, then tapers to the right above the walls of the Shipton Col. On the right-hand skyline, the summit of Changabang's gentler though taller sister, Kalanka, 22 741 ft.

On top of that the rock's permanently covered with fresh snow which would make progress on the ridges even more laborious.

It looks as if our only chance of climbing Changabang is up the back from the Changabang Glacier. So we're now established on the wrong glacier, and it would take three or four days to go back and get on to the Changabang Glacier from below. Or we could cut straight over the steep wall ahead of us—the Shipton Col—then go down to the head of the Changabang Glacier. This involves hard climbing and a lot of jumaring up fixed ropes so it's out of the question for the porters. So it would have to be a lightweight Alpine-style push with the climbers carrying all their gear. We argue around the problem and finally decide to go for the Col. Anyway it's more satisfying on aesthetic grounds to make a single committing push.

Martin:

May 21st. My first sighting of Changabang was not a happy occasion. The view was certainly magnificent, the mountain undoubtedly beautiful, but I felt disheartened. Our proposed route, the West Ridge, looked quite impossible; with tedious regularity the weather turned nasty around mid-day; I was struggling to acclimatise. I was panting like a dying dog in a state of imminent collapse even when I was just creeping up a gentle grass slope. How the hell would I manage on overhanging rocks?

Back in England we had casually picked out a likely route on faded and vintage photographs. What had looked there like a classic line now revealed itself as one vast slab of milky granite interrupted only by the occasional huge overhang. The nearer we approached, the more obvious it became: we were on the wrong side of the mountain. Chris, optimistic to the last, thought it might be easier 'round the corner'. Doug, losing sight of reality, muttered about 'the glorious challenge of big wall climbing'. But Dougal and I were already weighing up the prospects of crossing Shipton's Col.

The east face offered an obvious possibility up easier angled snow and ice. If the weather showed no signs of improving, we would not be able to climb technically difficult rock. It was too late to change valleys—this would involve several days' march in any case. Our only reasonable alternative was to cross the Col. Eric Shipton had already been to the Col from the other side, from the Changabang Glacier, but he had been put off descending to the Rhamani. This was hardly surprising as the Col drops very steeply—vertical and overhanging crag for 600 feet, icy but still steep for another 800 feet. It was not going to be easy.

Hank:

The decision about the route was disappointing. Everyone's mind had been set on the idea of the West Ridge, hoping it would afford an opportunity to expand their experience of high-standard rock climbing at high altitude. Doug and Martin, the hard rock experts, were particularly looking forward to this, and the Indians were looking forward to learning a great deal about a kind of mountaineering that was unfamiliar to them. But conditions put both the West Ridge and the South Ridge out of the question—they were formidably steep, they were coated with ice, and the weather was uncertain.

The first priority was to climb the mountain. They had to go for the route that offered the best chance of success. And this meant forcing access to the east face. The key to this was the Shipton Col.

6. The Climbing Begins

1. Crossing the Shipton Col

Who would make the route over the Shipton Col? With the spat at Deodi still fresh in every mind, they made the decision by drawing straws and Doug and Martin won. Dougal did not hide his disappointment. 'Dougal was not enthusiastic at the prospect of us mere mortals going out in front,' wrote Doug; while Martin reported that he 'could detect a touch of frustration in Dougal's normally impeccable manner—he is not, temperamentally, support-team material.'

Eric Shipton had approached the Col that bears his name from the other side, gained the notch which marks the lowest point of the ridge, and looked down at the Rhamani Glacier to find himself 'separated from it by a vertical wall of rock whose smooth face it was quite impossible to descend.'

This was the face that Martin and Doug now had to climb. There seemed two possible ways. The direct approach, favoured by Martin, would take them up an obvious snow ramp and along a rightward traverse to the foot of the rocky head wall which they would then have to climb by one of its crack systems. The other possibility, longer and more devious, would mean scaling an ice wall half a mile to the south, then traversing along the crest of the ridge until they reached the notch. Dougal considered this the likeliest route.

The first job now was to establish Advance Base Camp at the head of the Rhamani Glacier, about 18 000 feet above sea level. By mid-day on May the 22nd Doug and Martin were settled there in a two-man tent.

Martin:

'We ought to walk over to the Col and have a look,' Doug suggested.

I agreed reluctantly—it was a bit of a waste lying here all afternoon. We shouldered heavy rucksacks, plodded through thick wet snow across the Glacier and up the lower slopes. It was an infuriating walk without a great deal of point. We could see very little and to make matters worse I was trailing Doug all the way. 'Come on youth—get a move on. What's keeping you?' Doug at his blunt and irritating best! His remarks did, I suppose, stir up a bit of anger which kept me going up the last tedious slope to the foot of the climbing. We returned immediately and we agreed that I should cook evening meals if Doug would cook breakfasts.

It was odd in some ways that Doug and I should be teamed up. Before the expedition we hardly knew one another. We had of course been bumping into each other for years—ever since I started climbing—but our relationship had always been tentative and wary. We are in many ways very different. Doug is a Nottingham man, involved with his city, and proud of it. I have shifted around more and have never felt any particular loyalty to places or institutions. Doug is a 'club man', I am much more a loner. Doug has always shown a predilection for artificial climbing, I have always tried to avoid it. The expedition had thrown us together and surprisingly we seemed to get on together although our friendship was not without its teething troubles. Doug readily accepts new ideas, he is prone to 'enthusiasms', his latest conversion having taken place on the road to Yosemite. He found me disconcertingly cynical.

I woke up relieved to see Doug, clad in woolly hat and mittens, furiously pumping a primus stove. The luxury of bed tea—followed by the pain of frozen boots. We got off in good time and it was with relief that I discovered I was fit at last. We quickly reached our dump of equipment and started to solo up the snow slope behind. We reached a rocky slab which barred the way to our snow band. Neither of us wanted to ask for a rope but it was soon obvious that one was required. As always in such situations the rope was finally put on when we were both gripped, teetering on crampon points in a highly precarious situation. It was an awkward pitch but the climbing ahead was easier. It involved a long upward traverse on snow and ice which would bring us out at the bottom of the rock head wall. The traverse took us much longer than we expected, the hours slipped by, clouds piled in through the Rishi Gorge and our hopes of reaching the Col died.

Doug:

Having come up from the valley more or less continuously without a rest we both felt the altitude and at 19 000 feet moved ponderously through soft snow lying precariously on steep granite slabs. Shipton's photographs taken in September showed very little snow and almost continuously dry rock. Fifty-pound loads did not make the going any easier but for me at least who had hardly touched snow since Everest in 1972 it was pleasant to kick along the steepening band. Although after a year's rock climbing on North American granite it was frustrating not to climb at least some of the beautiful white Changabang granite. Day after day we were to find the only viable chinks in our mountain defences up ice and snow faces. When we arrived five hundred feet below the notch it was obvious that to climb the vertical and overhanging rock would have taken several days. So we descended, leaving seven hundred feet of rope fixed down slabs of rock to the left of a steep ice couloir.

We thought that perhaps the quickest solution would be to climb up

29. The Shipton Col posed a serious problem. On their first attempt Doug and Martin climbed the snow fields that slope up from left to right in the centre of the picture, but were turned back by the steep head wall.

on to the ridge further south by a snow and ice face and then traverse along the crest of the ridge to the notch. From there we could drop ropes down to our previous high point and continue down to the glacier.

We had just worked out a route after returning from the first attempt when Ujagar and Karin arrived hot-foot from the forested valleys and the frustrations of urging unwilling porters along to Base Camp. They were both naturally keen on some action. Next morning, however, Ujagar was feeling sick either with a bug or simply because he had gained height too fast. Karin too thought he had better take things easy to acclimatise more readily.

Martin:

I felt weary but determined next morning. We were away by 6 a.m., heading for a large ice face which led up to the ridge which was continuous with the Col. Our route was not without danger. Earlier I had observed avalanches fall and any route we chose would involve travers-

30. At the top of the snow field, Martin studies the problems of the head wall.
31. Martin prospecting the head wall.

ing below large seracs. The snow was fortunately well frozen but we did not have long before the sun would arrive on it. There was no question of roping up, this would have slowed us down too much. The slope was steep but I was going well. This time I was the fittest, and out in front—perhaps I was more frightened than Doug.

We reached a line of seracs and it was frightening to see the fractured and honeycombed cliffs at close quarters. I climbed with manic energy until I was clear of their fall line, just in time for we were now bathed in hot sun. Above was the final slope, steep and on deteriorating snow. I now felt extremely tired but it was difficult to rest until at least I reached the crest. There was no view; the clouds had already arrived. I slumped down away from the cornice and waited for Doug.

Doug:

The glistening green slivers of ice stayed in place as we passed beneath them and out of their line of fire. The snow steepened to sixty degrees and was reduced to a thin three-inch veneer over hard ice. A rope would have relieved the tension I felt at that point especially as Martin had left very little snow on which to stand. After backing up slightly right of his steps I collapsed on to the ridge.

Martin:

He joined me, muttering darkly. He rummaged in his sack to find the long-promised fruit juice.

'Christ, you stupid bugger, you've brought the tinned mashed potatoes!' I hurled mine away gaining only a little satisfaction from the act. Doug stolidly munched through his—and even offered me some.

We roped up and began the long and tedious traverse. The first section was along a narrow, heavily-corniced ridge. The snow was in bad condition, lumps of cornice repeatedly fell off. We decided which way we would leap if it came away under us. We thankfully gained a rocky section but this involved ups and downs and it in turn was plastered with appallingly soggy snow which had to be kicked off. We reached a gendarme and had to abseil down and round it. We were both beginning to tire alarmingly and this showed itself in bad-tempered exchanges. We had difficulty in agreeing on the route but the second man had little say in the matter. We climbed together for the most part, threading the rope around rock spikes, hoping no-one would fall. A short hard rock pitch emphasised the difficulty of climbing at 20 000 feet.

We eventually reached a col of sorts and anxiously peered into the misty depths below. We tried to convince ourselves that we had arrived, Doug more successfully than I.

'Let's wait till the mists clear.'

'Wait till the mists clear! If they do clear it will be midnight and what will we do then?' I replied icily.

I pushed on ahead, *à cheval* along a wafer ridge, and down some soggy snow. Lumps kicked off would trigger wedge-shaped avalanches which hissed and slithered down to the Glacier. We came at last to a recognisable feature, a huge rock 'gargoyle' overlooking a notch in the ridge. Our Col must be the next one but to get to it we had to abseil down and lose five hundred precious feet. Doug stamped a trail across rotten snow to a gully which finally brought us there. We were still beset by doubt, however, if it was the right col, and we would be hard pressed to get down.

We tied together all our ropes and hurled them off. I wanted to go first but Doug insisted. Didn't he trust me to fix a rope? He disappeared down into the mist. I shouted after him but I had to wait several troubled minutes before I received the comforting reply. I tugged the rope to test if he was off it and up thundered a string of obscenities and orders to 'get off the rope'.

'Hello!' A voice, distinctly Kiran's, floated through the mist. Was he waiting for us?

32. The mountain on the left is Rishikot. Its steep West Face, in sunlight, was the scene of Chris and Dougal's one-day attempt.

We reached the bottom but there was no Kiran. He called again and this time we looked up and saw a figure in the ragged mists. He was half way across yesterday's ice traverse. What the hell was he doing? Where was Ujagar?

'Are you O.K.?'

'Yes.'

'Well come back down.'

We looked on in horror, helpless for we were not in any shape to give much assistance.

'Do you need help?' we forced ourselves to ask.

Apparently he didn't and it was with relief that we watched him slowly retrace his steps. We walked back uneasily, with many backward glances. He had got back most of the way but he was now almost stationary. We got to camp and despatched Ujagar to render assistance. If help was needed he could call us. We settled down to rest awhile, to have a brew, to wait as darkness approached.

Doug:

We collapsed on to our pits and slowly began to remove double boots and all the other paraphernalia before settling in for the night.

At about 9 p.m. we heard an anguished cry for help. 'Shit' and 'fuck', he said or I said, and it was back into double boots and the now frozen gaiters and anoraks, and away across the two or three miles to the ramp. But after only half a mile we met Ujagar who said he felt ill. We sent him back to the camp and reached the foot of the ramp, expecting to find Kiran's body. We were sick with worry as there were no answers to our shouts and no sign of a body either. Then, from the direction of the camp came Kiran's voice. We staggered back not amused to find Kiran had broken another trail back from the face and had missed us in the dark. However, any feelings of ill temper quickly evaporated when we heard of his narrow escape.

Martin:

Kiran staggered a little and was incoherent. We put him to bed and next morning feeling slightly better he told us his story. He had been going well when he dropped his ice axe. He had taken one crampon off to use it as a substitute ice axe but he fell off, bounced over the rock wall and down the three hundred feet of snow slope. He hit his head and tore some muscles in his shoulder.

Poor Kiran, so anxious to help, so full of energy, was now paying the price of his imprudent enthusiasm. It was to cost him the summit he had longed to climb.

2. Rishikot

Hank:

I had moved up in the wake of the others and arrived at Base Camp on the 21st, pleasantly surprised to find how safe and spacious and comfortable it was. Next day we all carried loads up to the site of Advance Base. In the brilliant sunlight, on the bright snow, the place was a glaring inferno. It seemed a moot point whether it would be more uncomfortable in good weather or bad.

Less acclimatised than the others, I rested a long time there, watching Doug start to dig out a level platform for their tent. Then I sauntered slowly down to Base Camp, to find Chris and Dougal fussing about their climbing gear in a state of barely suppressed excitement like two schoolboys planning some illegal escapade. It was not long before Chris blew the gaff. They had decided to have a go next day at Rishikot, the 21,000 foot peak that loomed above Base Camp. Chris had persuaded himself that it would be a good acclimatisation exercise.

Dougal:

You couldn't help seeing the face of Rishikot on the various ferries up and down to Advance Base. A big sprawling-looking mountain from Base Camp, it got better and better as you walked up towards Changabang till it apexed into an impressive ice face.

Chris and I were due for a rest. We'd been probing and ferrying for many days to get established at the foot of our elusive main objective. But we felt more like climbing than lying around for a day. Coming down from Advance Base the tempting ice wall of Rishikot set all kinds of thoughts going round my head. Chris is generally enthusiastic about any project that involves climbing so I casually brought out a thought that had been tossing around in my mind for a few days.

'How about trying to climb the face of Rishikot tomorrow?'

No hesitation. 'Great idea! You're on!'

It was interesting to see our minds at work. The normal idea on peaks of 20 000 feet and above is to set up camp and proceed to climb them methodically. But because of our combined experience of altitude climbing we now knew enough about our performances to feel we could attempt a serious face route on a big peak with a similar mental attitude to that involved in tackling a major Alpine face. Rishikot was simply a higher version of the same thing. In looks it resembled the North Face of the Lauterbrunnen Breithorn in the Bernese Oberland but we hoped to be able to avoid the rock ribs at the top and climb completely on ice.

Carefully working out our chances, we estimated that it could be done in a day if we travelled very light and climbed quickly. To take bivouac gear would have meant heavy packs and an automatic slowing down so we took an extra sweater, water bottle and some bars of chocolate. It was a finely-calculated gamble on an outside chance, as we had to be back in the Changabang action within a couple of days.

Chris:

May 23rd. What a day! Acclimatisation or exhaustion? We set out at one o'clock in the morning, just carrying down jackets and a bit of food. We only had one head-torch between us, so stumbled blindly over the glacier, reached the foot of the face at four, just as the eastern skyline began to lighten, silhouetting Changabang, black and spiky.

We climbed all day, most of it on a thin frightening covering of snow on hard ice—kick in with cramponed boots; step up gently, relying on the snow to hold; hammer in an ice piton every fifty feet or so—we were now moving slowly through the dawn up towards a golden line of sun-drenched snow that crept down towards us. Bitter cold suddenly turned to warmth as the sun hit us, but we didn't have the sun for long. Changabang was capped with a stack of clouds like inverted saucers that grew into a cluster of giant umbrellas. High clouds spread a grey scum across the sky above and by nine o'clock we were in cloud, snow gusting —but we kept climbing right through to five o'clock that evening.

Dougal:

The first part was straightforward on snow, but the sun popped over the ridge and made the steepening section ahead very avalanche-prone. Roping up, we trod carefully until the sun disappeared, but then the daily snowfall started even earlier than usual. The surface snow got thinner and thinner until we were left with the centre section in hard ice. Slow work as the axes and hammers didn't always stick. Then long pitches of rotten snow and hard ice, always in wind and snow and cloud but gaining height all the time. Around four in the afternoon we came out on to the summit icefield and particularly nasty ice conditions. It still looked a long way to the summit and blunted crampons and in-effectual picks made the going slower.

There was a bivouac looming high in our immediate futures. Neither of us was prepared to accept the risk. You don't treat a bivouac without gear above 20 000 feet lightly. We would have survived, the peak would have been climbed, but in all probability there might have been a visitation from frostbite. Frostbite would have meant the loss of Changabang and a serious blow to the expedition's chances. Such a small team couldn't afford to lose too many members.

Chris:

There was little discussion; we came to the same decision together—two hours of daylight left—we could see a slightly easier way down, turned round, and started down, still moving one at a time, but faster now we are no longer defying gravity: down, down, down. Little feeling of disappointment, just want to get back in one piece, very aware of how committed we are, even more aware of the numbing exhaustion.

We reached an ice wall just as it got dark; fumbled down ice blurred in the gloom; don't fall off now right at the end! We got down safely but we still had to get back across the glacier. Have I ever been so tired? Just keep moving; force yourself on, one step at a time. I stumble on loose scree, sit down. Will we never get back? But we did, at ten o'clock that night. We hadn't reached the top but it was good acclimatisation. More than that, it was an incredible day's climbing—tensed, exacting.

Dougal:

Despite failure, it was a valuable day. It showed us something about our level of fitness. We had done 7000 feet of difficult ascent and descent at altitude. Sure we were tired, but that kind of day in the Alps makes one pretty tired as well. More importantly it opened out new horizons in the treatment of difficult faces on medium-range high-altitude peaks which I'm sure was a psychological boost on our subsequent ascent of Changabang.

Hank:

At Base Camp we grew more and more worried as darkness fell and it began to look as if Chris and Dougal had been forced to make a high bivouac on Rishikot with their inadequate gear. The kitchen boys kept a brew constantly ready just in case they turned up. And it was a great relief when they finally staggered into camp, all right but exhausted. Dougal's quiet burr had diminished to a hoarse whisper and Chris was almost incoherent with weariness. 'God, I'm fucked!' Chris finally managed to gasp. 'Don't think I've been so shattered since . . . I can't remember when.' And a little while later, after he had drunk some tea and hot soup, he said, 'Christ, it's easy to underestimate these mountains!'

I had seen them both in the late morning when they were two tiny black dots on the massive white face of the mountain, moving with infinite circumspection but already more than half way up. The cliff above them looked steeper and more dangerous than the part they had already climbed and the weather, true to its daily custom, was beginning to close in. I was moved to wonder, not for the first time, what was the drive that could make men, otherwise perfectly sane and sensible, undertake an enterprise so uncomfortable and arduous and dangerous purely in the interests of a day's sport.

I appreciate the attractions of climbing at hospitable altitudes. Life offers few pleasures more intense or more rewarding than a day's rock climbing in the Lake District or North Wales. And I know, too, that snow and ice mountaineering in Scotland or the Alps can give hours of high delight to those who are prepared to stretch their muscles and nerves.

But the Himalayas are something else entirely. The dangers are great and generally of a kind—avalanches, crumbling ice cliffs, sudden changes in the weather—that threaten even the most careful and experienced of men. Someone worked out that the current death rate for Himalayan climbers is one in eight—every eight climbers, that is, who go above Base Camp must expect to lose one of their group. It is a frightening statistic and some climbers think it is unduly pessimistic, but there is no doubt that the dangers are great in the Himalayas—of serious injury as well as of death—and the chances of rescue or speedy access to full medical help are not good. And everyone who goes climbing at 20 000 feet and above must accept, as a matter of course, a good deal of physical discomfort: extremes of temperature with the threat of frostbite; splitting headaches and insomnia; nausea and vomiting; constipation or dysentery and/or piles; exhaustion intensified by the lack of oxygen, which makes the simplest task a matter for hard and patient effort; hunger sometimes, and thirst and dehydration; a sore throat and a recurrent cough and bouts of gasping for breath even when immobile, all the pains of acclimatisation, and the ever-present fear of the killer diseases, pulmonary oedema and pneumonia. It is a nasty catalogue, and in addition to all this the Himalayan mountaineer must expect to have to do much more hard and tedious slogging than actual climbing. Most of the time he is simply trudging up steep places with a heavy load on his back.

So why do they do it? Why do they persist in doing it? The question is asked continuously and never satisfactorily answered. The drive is clearly a strong one. Perhaps its roots are too deep and personal and private to permit any simple rational explanation. Perhaps in the end the only possible reply, though this is not satisfactory either, is the one Louis Armstrong gave to the man who asked him what jazz was: 'If you have to ask, you'll never know.'

3. Walking back

I had to leave them on May the 25th and set off home. My editor had given me one month off and that meant I had to be back in the office in London by June the 1st. So I was cutting it pretty fine anyway—two days for the walk down to the road, two more for the journey to Delhi by truck and train, and two for the flight to London. If nothing went wrong, I would just make it.

It was a strange mixed-up feeling to be leaving everyone. I was sad to be going just as the real climbing was beginning but I was also looking forward, with a sneaking selfishness, to getting back to my family and all the civilised comforts that you take for granted until you have to manage without them—a hot bath and clean clothes, chairs to sit in and a bed to sleep on, salads and fresh fruit and long cold drinks.

The day began inauspiciously. I needed to be away from Base Camp by ten in the morning because I wanted to reach the woods of Dibrugheta by nightfall. After breakfast I collected piles of letters and rolls of film from everyone and sorted out my gear and packed my rucksack and briefcase. Then I sat in the sun to wait for Doug and Martin who were coming down from Advance Base with film of their attempt on the Shipton Col which I wanted to take back to ITN. But it was not until ten-thirty that they appeared on the moraine ridge above us and then I had to hear the story of their climb and Kiran's fall. So it was after eleven when I finally waved goodbye to everybody and set off for temporary base camp, feeling very small and lonely and wishing I could stay till the end of the expedition.

An hour later at the lower camp I found Pansing, the porter who had been detailed to help carry my gear down to the road. He took my briefcase and slung it with a kitbag on to his back and set off up the hill. I followed him slowly and at the top of the slope, just before the path dipped again and swung eastwards at the start of the long contouring route above the Rishi Gorge, I paused for a farewell look at the sand-coloured spire of Changabang.

I had not been looking forward to this solitary walk back. But it turned out to be idyllic. I was fit enough now, once I found a rhythm, to move steadily and reasonably fast without any sense of strain. The load in my rucksack, thirty-five pounds or so, felt perfectly manageable. The weather was unusually good—there was a brief snow flurry in the early afternoon but then the clouds moved on and the sun shone again. And Pansing, one of the more villainous-looking of the porters, proved to be the perfect companion, sure of the path and enviably sure-footed, continuously considerate and cheerful. There was no conversation. Apart from a few basic words—'achha' for 'good', 'Tikh hai?' for 'All right with you?', 'rasta' for 'path' and, of course, 'cigarette'—we had no common language. To all intents and purposes I was alone in the sunshine among some of the most splendidly dramatic mountain country in the world.

It was only eight or nine days since I had walked up that way, some sections more than once, but now every stage and detail burst upon me with the force and freshness of a new experience—the rough ridge path among the prostrate junipers, the smooth water-worn rock gullies, the continuous background roar of the white water of the Rishi a thousand feet below, the elaborate cairns, the wide field of gigantic tumbled blocks of granite, then the Big Wall that had loomed so ominously above us on the approach march. It was like coming across old, half-forgotten friends again.

The Deodi camp site had a sad air. We had stayed there for three or four days on the way up and it had begun to feel like a home. Now the lovely little clearing in the birches was deserted with only a few nostalgic reminders of its former bustle, the dry stone wall the cooks had built around the kitchen area, small piles of empty cans and broken crates and scraps of paper.

We stopped briefly for a cigarette, then shouldered our loads again for the last part of the day's march, the beautiful path that winds among the ridges and brings you to Dibrugheta. It was evening now. My feet were beginning to ache, the rucksack felt heavy and cumbersome and the way seemed much longer than I remembered it. At last we reached the woods and scrambled down the last few hundred feet to the camp site clearing. I threw my rucksack to the ground and started to unpack my sleeping bag. But Pansing had other ideas. He indicated that there was a much better place just a few minutes further on. I tried to make it clear to him that I was quite happy where I was. But he insisted. So, cursing him in my mind, I picked up the rucksack once more and stumbled after him, down a steep slope, across a river, up the other bank which was steep and slippery and seemed interminable, across a meadow, into the woods again and finally to the spot he had in mind. Of course, he was right. It was a perfect place—a few feet above a river a massive rock formed a low natural cave with a floor of soft leaf mould and plenty of room for us to pile our gear under cover and stretch out in sheltered comfort.

I eased my boots off and rubbed my protesting feet and wriggled down into the sleeping bag. Within a few minutes Pansing had a fire blazing at the entrance to the cave and a brew of tea on the way. It tasted like nectar, whatever that may taste like. I had eaten nothing since breakfast and the meagre supper, a tin of sardines and five or six biscuits, was marvellous.

Then I lay back, exhausted and utterly comfortable, to smoke a cigarette. The river roared past just below us and the logs crackled on the fire. The air was clean and scented with pine. For the first time for many nights my feet felt really warm. I contemplated the conifer branches high above, sharply etched against the evening sky, then gradually growing muzzy at the edges until they merged into the darkness.

It was a long time before sleep came and it did not matter. Occasionally one or other of us would reach over and throw another log on to the fire for the pleasure of watching the pale flames leap and lick around it as the sparks flew upwards.

It was my forty-eighth birthday and the strangest and one of the best I have ever had.

4. Fixed ropes and quick tempers

Meanwhile, back on the Rhamani Glacier, the way now lay open to the foot of Changabang itself. Martin and Doug had cracked the Shipton Col and placed their ropes and returned to Base Camp for a rest. Chris and Dougal and Ballu took over from them at Advance Base to tackle the next job—moving enough gear to the top of the Col to make the summit push possible.

Chris:

Dougal, Ballu and I set out for Advance Base on May the 26th. Dougal had left before us and by the time Ballu and I arrived he was comfortably installed in one of the tunnel tents and had a primus roaring.

So Ballu and I occupied the other tent and shared one for the rest of the expedition. I think this did more than anything to promote the friendship and understanding we built up over the next few weeks, which was undoubtedly a major factor in the happy relations that existed throughout the expedition.

33. Early morning at Advance Base.

Dougal never ceases to surprise me. I knew he could be relied on to work flat out on the mountain, particularly when out in front making the route, but in camp he tends to sit back with the philosophy that there are others who are both better at administrative chores than he is and who enjoy them anyway. But now there were just the three of us, Dougal settled into the tent with all the cooking equipment and for the next three days—until our cook caught up with us—fed us with a succession of excellent meals. In camp Ballu and I lay back, ate, read and played endless games of chess at which we were quite evenly matched though Ballu had the greater finesse and would gain checkmate by the occasional spectacular coup.

Our first task was to sort out the line of rope that Martin and Doug had dropped from the Col and establish a fixed rope up which it would be easy to ferry our supplies.

We set out at six on the morning of the 27th. Dougal, as always, was out in front so it naturally fell to him to clear the ice off the ropes. Ballu went next and I showed him the method of climbing fixed ropes. He had done it once before at an international training meet I had attended in

Kashmir the previous year. There had been two French climbers at the meet and they had taught him their way of climbing fixed ropes. This differs slightly from our method and so the unfortunate Ballu was rather confused. Furthermore, it is one thing to climb a fixed rope up a fifty-foot crag at only ten thousand feet above sea level, and quite another to struggle up a rope stretched diagonally across ice-plastered slabs at around 18 500 feet. It was a tribute to Ballu's determination and agility that he got up at all.

I couldn't help worrying, though, about how Ballu and the other Indians were going to react to this kind of climbing. We spent the day sorting out the ropes, improving the line, so that they went straight down a steep ice gully that led directly to the Col. The final three hundred feet was up a bulging head wall in a single run out. Dougal went up it first, pulling out a long stretch of rope and then moving very slowly and laboriously as he cleared the rope of ice—unless you do this, the little teeth of the jumar clamp become gummed with ice and the clamp starts slipping, a frightening experience when you are over a thousand feet up.

I followed Dougal, while Ballu waited at the foot of the final steep section. It was like Chamonix granite with a crack splitting the rock wall that was just too wide for hand jamming, clean cut and straight, its sides coated in ice. I wasn't surprised that Martin and Doug had opted for the long way round.

The top was a narrow notch—just wide enough to squeeze through. Cloud was now swirling round the summits of Changabang and Kalanka but we could see down to the Changabang Glacier, and across to the great icefall cascading down to the Kalanka-Changabang Face. Dougal had dropped down the snow gully that ran easily down the Changabang Glacier side of the Col. I contented myself with examining the lower slopes of the Kalanka Face. These were guarded by a series of inter-linking serac walls. You could see the avalanche debris scattered on the glacier below. But there seemed to be a route up a rock arête towards a stable serac, a short steep ice wall, a gangway and then a long snow ramp that led into the clouds. A distant roar; plume of ice crystals and an avalanche careered down the Face, but well to the left of the line I had picked.

Dougal returned—he'd picked the same line. We plummeted back down our fixed ropes. On the way down I put in extra anchor-points to make the journey back up easier.

We returned to the Col early the following day, to ferry up some more gear and to have a better look at the Kalanka Face. This time Ballu came all the way to the Col, slow and laborious and determined, and he got there in the end. Meanwhile, Dougal and I had dropped down the other

34. Chris, secured to the fixed rope by two jumar clamps, arrives at the top of the Shipton Col with a load of supplies for the summit push.
35. The struggle with heavy loads up the fixed ropes on Shipton Col.

side. It was only seven in the morning but the Changabang Glacier side faced south-east and got the full blast of the early morning sun. The snow, which was lying on smooth slabs, was already dangerously sugary. Avalance tracks were an uncomfortable reminder of just how dangerous this slope could be. We dropped down about six hundred feet to the top of a small gully. We had no rope with us and the snow lay in an all-too-thin layer over the rock so we decided we had gone far enough. It was a brilliantly clear morning and we could examine the Face in detail. There was definitely a route winding its way through the serac walls. It wasn't completely free from objective danger, but at least the risks would be acceptable—and so we returned, getting back at midday. That afternoon Doug, Martin and Tashi arrived with two of our cook boys. Advance Base was truly established.

That night we discussed the plan. Next day we should make a carry to the Col of all the gear and food we would need for the next eight days. We would then have a rest day and on the day after we would move over to the Changabang Glacier, picking up the loads on the Col and carrying them down to a camp at the foot of the Face. We would then be on our own—there would be no-one left at Advance Base who could possibly cross the Col in support or in the event of an emergency.

The question was, how many should take part in the push for the summit? I favoured a party of six, since this was a compact number, could squeeze into two tents on the final push, and climb in two ropes. There were eight climbers altogether, but Ujagar was definitely out of the running. He had gone up to the foot of the fixed ropes that morning, but had complained of feeling sick and returned to the camp. He was now talking of going back to Base Camp. Kiran, also, was a doubtful starter—his shoulder was still giving trouble. And Tashi's condition was worrying for he still complained of bad piles. None of these three had yet been on the fixed ropes and Ballu was only just getting the hang of jumaring.

That night I had that slightly tense feeling one gets before a committing climb. I was worried by the unknown quantities we were faced with, particularly the performance of the Indian members of the team. It was important that more than one Indian climber should reach the summit, but the kind of ascent we were contemplating was particularly serious—should any member of the team fall sick and want to turn back, everyone else would have to accompany him. I slept badly that night, my mind over-active, weighing up all the pros and cons.

Next morning we were preparing to make our big carry to the Col—Martin, Doug, Dougal, Ballu, Tashi and myself. I was tired and irritable and was packing my sack for the slog ahead when Ballu, who was carrying the paraffin for our stoves, complained that he couldn't stop the can leaking. Somehow this sparked off all my worry and I let rip into Ballu about the failure of the Indians to get our butane gas from Bombay in time for us to have it on the mountain. This was particularly unfair on Ballu since it hadn't been his responsibility and he knew nothing of the delay. I then stormed off, dissipating very little of my temper in the effort of walking, barely conscious of the magnificent monolith of Changabang and the great sweep of the Rhamani Glacier cirque.

Ballu was unwise enough to overtake me about two-thirds the way across to the foot of the Col. I had been balancing out in my mind the various permutations of climbers to ensure success in our summit push and I'm afraid let rip at Ballu once again as he caught up with me. The blow-up was, more than anything else, simply a way of relieving my stress, and it was a tribute to the friendship the two of us had built up that the anger could subside as fast as it had swelled.

Ballu:

Chris and I had an explosion on the mountain during a heavy carry on May 29th. There were just the two of us, fortunately, weighed under our heavy loads. At this stage I was the only Indian climber who was, to quote Chris, 'going like a bomb'. Tashi was fighting his piles, Ujagar Singh was out of the climb, and Kiran had got hurt. I had sent the doctor, DJ Singh, a note asking him when, if at all, any of these climbers would be fit to come up. Tashi had come up the previous day and had fitted in with Martin and Doug. I was keen that Kiran, who had done so much to organise the expedition, should have a crack at the mountain, and suggested to Chris that if he came up today I would take him up on the ropes so that he could cross over with us a day later. Couldn't we put off the crossing of the Col for one day? Chris exploded, his angered vision ranging from the total collapse of the expedition to the British climbers going to the top on their own. I kept silent and took the precaution of getting ahead of Chris, who had to stretch his pace to keep me within range of his barrage. Lack of breath soon silenced him. We continued climbing and in the tent, that evening, Chris apologised: 'I am bloody irritable in the mornings, Ballu. Even Wendy has learnt never to make a suggestion in the early morning.' We later discussed the issue in detail and without heat.

36. Above Advance Base, the cirque of mountains at the head of the Rhamani Glacier. On the left, Dunagiri commands the western side. The small peak, just right of the centre of the picture, is Bagini Peak, 20 211 ft.

Chris:

That night Ballu and I talked over the plan for the next few days and agreed that we could not delay our final assault to wait for Kiran's shoulder to recover. The weather was very unsettled already. With an injured shoulder, and not having made an ascent of the fixed ropes already, Kiran could easily get himself into severe difficulties either on the route up to the Col or on any stretches that might require a fixed rope on the way up the Kalanka Face.

We decided that we should have a rest day the following day, since Dougal, Ballu and I had now made three successive trips to the Col, and on May 31st we should set out for the Changabang Glacier.

5. Bagini Peak

Doug and Martin ferried loads to the Col on May 29th but for three days before that they had been resting at Base Camp, so they felt fit and ready for some action on the official rest day. Inspired, perhaps, by the Chris/Dougal attempt on Rishikot, they plotted a little side-show of their own.

Martin:

We returned from our carry to the Col quite late but it had not been a particularly arduous day—more frustrating than anything, slowly jumaring up, literally hanging about for hours. Tomorrow was to be an 'official' rest day before we all shifted camp over Shipton's Col. But Doug and I were already rested. We had just spent three days lounging at Base Camp, and I felt ready for some action. That night I asked Doug if he fancied climbing the lovely little 20,200 foot peak at the head of the Glacier.

'Are you serious?'
'Why ever not?'
'But you'll have to get up early.'
'Not too early, surely?'
'Up by 3 a.m., away by five. Mamdu—bed tea 3 a.m.'
'Achha sir, you give me anorak end of expedition?'
'Ask Chris.'
'Already try, he tell me try Doug.'

Mamdu, a Kashmiri and a splendidly cheerful high-altitude porter, was a persistent and wily scrounger. But bed tea arrived on time and we got away soon after five.

Doug:

At 5.30 a.m. the brilliant blue sky, still cold air and crisp crunchy snow had all the makings of a perfect day out. We worked our way along snow-covered moraine before cutting across directly to a promin-

37. Martin on Bagini Peak—'frosty cold snow brought momentarily to life, lit up like a hundred diamond sparks'.

ent ridge. As we crossed the glacier new aspects of the surrounding mountains revealed themselves. We now had a full frontal view of the mighty East Face of Dunagiri. It was, from our position, a beautifully proportioned mountain with granite aiguilles rising up on both flanks of the symmetrical summit—a summit that dominates this part of the Garhwal just as Nanda Devi stands proud of all the other peaks to the south-east. As we gained height on the lower flanks of our mountain, the ice-fluted double summit of Nanda Devi appeared from behind the Shipton Col. We zig-zagged up steeper ground, urged on as much by our curiosity to see more of Nanda Devi and the neighbouring peaks as by our climb.

The sun was by now shining down from over the West Ridge of Changabang. It slanted across the undulating snow—frosty cold snow brought momentarily to life, lit up like a hundred diamond sparks in the penumbra of light. Every facet of the snow crystals seemed to shimmer rainbow colours for as long as the sun's light skimmed the surface of the snow.

We were in no hurry and Martin for once was pleased to join me in long rests, contemplating the peaks as they grew to full stature. We planned euphorically to climb everything we could see and to cross all the cols on distant watersheds. But as so often happens the best-laid plans terminate after the major commitment has been completed and in our case, after climbing Changabang, there was little enthusiasm for anything other than to scurry off home.

Martin:

The views were staggering. We revelled in the beauty, and whooped with joy at being alive. It was a morning when you pitied those who were still in bed. The sun rose behind Changabang and silhouetted most dramatically the huge West Face, one enormous sweep of vertical and overhanging rock, plated here and there by ludicrously steep ice. The route we had originally contemplated was obviously so difficult it was laughable.

We reached a rocky section of the ridge and it proved far more awkward than expected. Doug led off round an awkward step and we were surprised to find a little cairn on top. I recalled reading an account by André Roch of his solo attempt on a peak next to Changabang—

38. The formidable South-West Face of Changabang seen from half-way up Bagini Peak. In the distance, in the sun, the twin summits of Nanda Devi.

39. From high up on Bagini Peak, the North Face of Nanda Devi towers above the walls of the Shipton Col. The main peak, centre of picture, was first climbed by Tilman and Odell in 1936, from the other side of the mountain. At 25 645 ft, it was the highest point reached by men on foot. Nanda Devi East, to the left, was climbed in 1939. The ridge from the East Peak to main peak remains one of the most haunting of Himalayan challenges. It was attempted in 1951 by a French team but their two lead climbers failed to return from the ridge and their bodies were never found.

presumably this marked his high point. I could understand his reluctance to solo further for the ridge rose steeply ahead and it was of hard ice.

We stopped at the last resting site and Doug pulled out two tins of juice.

'You absolute cretin, you've done it again!' Once more a tin of potatoes is viciously flung into the eternal snows. Doug is almost moved to apologise but thinks better of it, and proceeds to munch without obvious relish.

Doug:

By now the sun was making the surface snow mushy and so we belayed on ice pegs, cutting steps now and again to help with the descent, taking turns to lead. We were on the summit by noon, enveloped in thick mist. We could only catch brief glimpses of the Bagini Glacier system and the huge 7000-foot North-West Face of Changabang. This stupendous slice of rock was in part plastered with hard green water ice that seemed to have been glued in position by the strong winds for parts of it were wrapped round overhangs and stuck across huge open slabs of white rock.

We quickly retraced our steps down the ridge and sauntered back across the upper Rhamani Glacier to reach camp for afternoon tea. It had been a perfect day out in these incomparable mountains.

7. The Summit

1. The summit push begins

The final push towards the summit began in the early hours of May the 31st. From now on most of the climbing would be done at night.

Successive ferries up the fixed ropes had established a sizable dump at the top of the Shipton Col, the material for five days in the promised land of 'total commitment'—three two-man tents, food, cooking equipment, ropes and climbing ironmongery, film and cameras and books and a pocket chess set. The plan now was to jumar up the ropes, move the loads down the other side of the Col to camp at the head of the Changabang Glacier about 19 000 feet above sea level, then climb northwards towards the col between Changabang and Kalanka to establish a top camp as near as possible to the South-East Ridge of Changabang.

From now on they would be on their own. From Advance Base onwards there was no possibility of anyone else or any further supplies coming up to help them. If anything went wrong, if anyone was injured, they would have to struggle back as best they could. Anything they could not carry, they would have to do without.

The composition of the summit party was determined by events. Neither Kiran nor Ujagar was fit enough to go, and neither of them had acquired the jumaring skill that would be needed. So the final party would consist of the four British climbers who were all going well, and two of the Indians, Ballu who was in fine form and Tashi who was still suffering from piles but had determined to master them in the Haston fashion, by carrying on as if they were not there.

Chris:

May 31st. The start of the big push. The cook boy called us at midnight. Flurries of cloud were chasing the moon but Changabang was clear. We set out at intervals of about an hour each, Dougal first to clear the ropes, then the rest of us, to avoid waiting around on the fixed ropes.

Dougal:

I left Advance Base at midnight on my usual rope-clearing task. Once again it was difficult, involving constant use of one and sometimes two Hieblers to supplement the slipping jumars. Usually a three-hour journey, it wasn't until 5 a.m. that I reached the Col. With the clear ropes the others were close behind and we loaded up heavily with the equipment dumped there and started quickly down the other side before the sun turned the avalanche-prone slope to a dangerous mush.

Ballu:

Dougal leaves at midnight and I follow at 1 a.m. (May 31st). At the base of the wall I put on my crampons. Front-pointing and using the short ice axe for fifty feet and the first rope is there. Clip one jumar on and, still on front-points and axe, another fifty feet are covered. Second jumar is clipped and I jumar up, stamping my crampons. I get to the next rope. If the front climber is still on the rope—and Dougal out in front has the toughest job, going first and having to clear all the ice that has formed on the ropes—then you stay on your rope, belayed and out of the way of snow and ice being dislodged from above, and try to keep from freezing until you can get on to the next rope. Hunks of ice clatter down. Some of them bounce off my crash hat and a few of the venturesome ones are down my back and I feel rather wet. My feet and hands get numb.

Two ropes up I hear Dougal hammering ice off the rope and soon I see the pencil point of his head torch. I follow his progress by the light. I climb blind—my torch would not fit my crash hat and I can't breathe if I hold it in my mouth all the time. In the dark I cross my safety karabiner with one of the jumars while transferring from one rope to another; remove one glove; hold the torch in my mouth—nearly gives me osculatory frostbite; with numb fingers the errant karabiner is un-clipped, the tape unravelled, the karabiner correctly reclipped below the two jumars; the torch goes back in the sack and it is up again. Right jumar up, right foot up, weight to the right; left jumar and left foot up. Three ropes—each 300 feet—gone. Dougal's voice comes float-ing down, 'Ballu, if I were you I'd come up slowly. The ropes are frozen and you will have to wait.' Sane, very sane. Dougal rarely talks during a climb and when he does it is sense.

I give myself a tie at the next anchor and become small. A continuous avalanche of chipped ice and snow courses down and past me. Next 500 feet are straight rock and overhung in places. *Vive la* artificial climbing!

Get the nylon sling over the crampons and test the stirrups for smooth movement. Dougal's moved on to the next rope so I clip on the rope above me. As I take slack and slide the jumars up, the rope stretches. Gives you an edgy feeling. I have all the slack and am air-borne. There is a hint of dawn and I can see Dougal against the sky, suspended some way between the mountain and the sky. The wind has caught his long hair, gives him a prophetic silhouette. The valley below is dark and I can see two points of light. Must be Tashi and Chris. Or is it Martin and Doug?

A heavy rucksack on my back, hands and feet numb with cold, and a vacant mind, hanging in mid-air at 19 000 feet negotiating an overhang. Left crampon hits a protrusion and I swing out—the heavy rucksack nearly turns me round. Fractionally I look back at a new face, a new dawn face of Dunagiri, and all the vacancy of mind is gone. Remember Frank Smythe? 'One is grateful to Providence for having designed a vision of the hills to lighten the dark passages of the mind.' And I am grateful—numb and frozen, tired and breathless, suspended like a blooming bat.

Dougal is up the last rope before I get to its base. This one is an easy short pitch. So look out—it's an easy short pitch and that makes widows. It is another fifteen minutes before I am on the ridge. Five a.m. It is a narrow ridge. I anchor myself and the rucksack. We dig out our respective loads—the ferry we did on the 29th—two cans of paraffin, two stoves, a tent, a rope. I fill my rucksack, put a plastic sheet on top— can't go around smelling like a hurricane lantern. Stuff my personal gear on top and the friendly rucksack is not a friend any more. I must be an Atlas carrying this down. I pile my camera on top and outside the rucksack—by some mischance there are no outside pockets—slip the anchor and a huge hoist has the rucksack on my back. It also sends the camera rolling off and I watch it disappear on to the Changabang Glacier. Wonder what went wrong? We plod off down a snow gully; the comby surface crunches intimately under the crampons and, slowly, top heavy, we plug down.

Chris.

As Tashi and I got ready to set out the clouds crept up the Glacier, engulfed us, and drowned the moon. It was savagely cold; threatening, in the opaque gloom, with snow merging into cloud. No sign of Changabang. We could have been anywhere —in the Cairngorms, the Alps, or even the Derbyshire Peak District on a winter's day. But we were committed now, Dougal was already on the fixed ropes somewhere in front in the cloud. We would have to follow.

The cloud cleared for a few minutes—a little pin-point of light half way up to the Col. It was now three thirty and the darkness was turning to predawn gloom. The cloud still threatened an angry dawn, ill omen for our attempt. Four of us gathered on the Col in the dawn and picked up the food and gear we had dumped the previous days. It meant carrying loads of around eighty pounds—desperately unwieldy but at least we were going down hill, over snow slopes which obviously lay on rock slabs and were prone to avalanche once the morning sun struck them.

It was only eight in the morning when we reached the head of the Changabang Glacier. Dougal had pushed on in front and had already found a good camp site, placing it very carefully to ensure that it was sheltered by a rock spur of Changabang from any big avalanche that could come off the face.

40. Tashi on his way up the Shipton Col, his jumar clamp attached to his waistline and securing him to the fixed rope.

41. The view down the fixed ropes on the Shipton Col.

Martin and Doug arrived about ten o'clock. They had left much later than us, tired from yesterday's climb, and as a result had a nerve-wracking descent of the now sugary snow on the Changabang Face of the Col. We lay all day in our tents stupified by the heat. An incredible contrast—from the cold of the night to the glaring heat of midday when the glacier becomes a huge reflector of the sun.

Dougal:

We sited the camp just on the side of a spur shielding us from potential ice fall from the long line of seracs on the Changabang Kalanka face. An impressive spot. Three small tents underneath Changabang and looking down past lesser but still impressive peaks to the skyline and Nanda Devi East and West with their sharply defined linking ridge, the traverse of which is on many climbers' minds.

2. Lousy interlude

Martin and Doug, after their strenuous rest day on Bagini Peak, were the last to leave Advance Base.

Doug:

At last it was time to pack and set off with everything in our sacks, turning our backs on the porters and cooks. After two weeks of walking and climbing we were rid of all the aches and pains of acclimatisation.

The unknown Ballu had proved to be a natural climber, and Tashi, too, had soon learned the knack of jumaring up to the Shipton Col. We were all in good humour, ready for an adventure we knew we could all share.

We shouldered more loads at the Col and dropped down the soft easy-angled snow to make camp on the Changabang Glacier. There we were stopped by the weather and had time to contemplate avalanches cascading down the face we had chosen to climb. Doubt and fear had time to germinate and swell into avalanche paranoia. But we all know everything will be fine once we are absorbed with the route. So we wait, as the avalanches rumble on.

Ballu:

I get my gear out and find it free of paraffin. Screw the bits of the pressure stove together, shovel some snow into a billy, light the stove and doze off. Twenty minutes and another shovelful of snow and another nap. Martin and Doug trudge in at mid-day, tired and burnt. A meal of soup, chicken stew and mashed potatoes. Lay the kit out to dry and back to sleep. A brew at five and a tuck of soup, stew and mashed potatoes, and strawberries. Dougal's mug and spoon are left at Advance Base. He uses a can for a mug-cum-plate and a rock peg for a spoon. Pack loads for the morrow and two games of chess with Chris. 'Start in the morning at 2 a.m.' 'Goodnight Chris'—and goodnight to all those the mind races to but dares not conjure up in this cold, cold world.

But it snows through the night and we stay in our sleeping bags.

Doug:

On the second morning I awoke after a night spent scratching at my crutch and armpits. I had felt uneasy for some time—ever since I had lent my sleeping bag to one of the porters. I was quite put out when I suddenly related my present discomfort to that act of misguided generosity. In the burning morning sun I stripped off. So that was it—translucent green creatures, with numerous twitching legs, running up the seams of my underpants, vest and jumper. They had been very busy breeding to judge by the number of tiny eggs piled up wherever it had been warmest.

'Ah, you've got lice,' said Ballu knowingly. 'We get them whenever we camp out with the local shepherds.'

Lice. I had often wondered what they looked like and now I knew. Being squeamish of that sort of thing, I took all my clothes off and began to crack them dead against my ice axe. I gave this up after I had only succeeded in clearing three inches of seam in half an hour. Martin, the biologist, reckoned that strong ultra-violet light should kill them. So, to Tashi's amusement, I stripped off down to my double boots and laid everything out on the snow.

Chris hovered about with his camera clicking, cursing his lack of

42. 'In the burning morning sun I stripped off.' Doug deals with his fellow-travellers.

foresight in not having his extension tubes to probe further into my misery. 'Take one for me,' yelled the others, as Chris demanded full frontal. 'Don't be shy. Go on—lift up your foreskin, you never know. . . .' Even Dougal stirred from his slumbers to get the cine camera in motion.

Ballu:

An unholy racket from the tunnel tent occupied by Martin and Doug. Some animal in the tent? Doug streaks out holding his long johns and looking keenly at the seams, alternately scratching his crotch and yelling 'Oh bloody hell!'

All of us now out of our slumber.

'Chris, what do lice look like? Is this one?'

'Yes, of course it is.' Chris is not so good at identifying fauna usually.

Doug's clothes are spread out on the snow. Glacier lassitude cured in a few minutes by a few lice. Are they the highest lice in the world? Will

they survive in this cold? Shouldn't Doug at least carry the poor eggs—
he finds some in his next-to-the-skin sweater—back? What about a
lice stew? In China they breed lice for eating. How fast can they walk?
Or do they jump while you sleep peacefully?

Martin has shared a tent with Doug for two weeks. He sits through all
this with typical British phlegm. Perhaps Doug's lice wouldn't hop on to
Martin without an introduction? 'Dr. Livingstone, I presume.' Anyway,
Martin's right; he has no lice.

3. To the top camp

Dougal:

There was much time to peruse the Face with eye and mind and
Chris and I took a wander up a small section to try and find a way
through the serac barrier.

A reasonable line was visible with a minimum of danger but would
definitely have to be tackled at night, making the ability to use the full
moon a very important factor in our planning. That is if it ever decided
to come out from behind the unfriendly cloud and give us some
assistance.

Morale was slightly on the slide during the day (June 2nd) as supplies
were having to be rationed and the larger appetites were beginning to
feel unsatisfied. There was talk of going back to Base for a few day's rest
and to pick up more supplies.

Ballu:

Our meals are skimpy. Packs made for the mountain are not to be
touched. By evening, though, we judiciously pinch food meant for high
camps and Martin and Tashi between them rig up a meal of soup, stew
and mashed potatoes. Low clouds and a smuggler's moon now and then.
We shall go up if the clouds lift by 9 p.m. If they don't it will be back to
Base to rest, sleep, eat and return for the ascent.

Dougal:

As we were reflecting and discussing that evening the clouds slipped
to lower valley level and we were left sipping tea in a surrealistic moonlit mountain scene with Changabang sticking up like one of Ludwig of
Bavaria's castles except instead of Wagnerian overtures, we had only the
sounds of our sceptical voices.

Would it last? Should we go?

We gave it an hour to consolidate but within half we were outside
once again, packing hurriedly. By 10 p.m. we were on the upward move
through the still soft snow.

It was a long, amazing, wonderful, impression-forming night. Devious route-finding. One pitch involving seven aid pegs and lots of front pointing in hard ice with the rustling powder sliding in the night wind. Feeling really well, I did most of the leading. The moon dipped and curved behind clouds and eventually dropped for the night in the middle of a front pointed pitch leaving me groping for a little before the pre-dawn glow asserted itself.

Ballu:

It is clear by 9 p.m. and we pack camp and leave. Clop, clop across the glacier and then up and up across deepening snow. We take turns ploughing ahead—quiet and determined. Midnight. Last of the clouds gone to roost: a brilliant moon. A 20–30 foot ice wall bars the way. It takes over an hour and five 'warthogs' until the first man is up. Cold feet. Thoughts of frostbite. Move front-pointing; running rope belays required more often. The moon sets at 3.30 and we can't see a thing. After ten minutes the mountain tops lighten and we are on the move again. More difficult ice/snow pitches. Feet getting colder. Dawn. Out of the cold night emerges Nanda Devi—like Neptune—now mauve, now gold—is this the face. . . . ? Yes, it is, it is. . . . Talking to my thoughts I am down in a snow trough. Pant and heave. Pant and heave and I lumber out. I now carry an extra rope, retrieved off the last pitch. I and my mind are dead with this unending walk and I forget to secure the rope to my harness and let it drag behind me. It is going to break my back. Nanda Devi, gold-tinged and imperial all the way to the twin peak, Nanda Devi East. Nanda Devi East is my love unrequited. I had sat out a week of snow and cold in 1964 there and had finally been avalanched off the mountain. There stand the twin peaks like a bride and a groom, linked by a castellated spur. Somewhere lie frozen and broken the two Frenchmen who tried the traverse in 1951. Surely the traverse would be the Blue Ribband of Himalayan climbing?

And that face again. The face of Troy. That face of Helen that launched a thousand mountains. Wrong? I can't remember the rest or the right. It's good to try one foot above the other. One gulp of air after another. Where has all the air gone? More light. Burning bright. Burning bright in the forests of the night. . . .

Martin:

We followed Dougal, hard put to keep to his giant strides. We were content to be led, down hill at first, over a lightly frozen stream and then uphill to a whaleback ridge of ice which led into a chaotic maze of ice pinnacles. This was as far as Chris and Dougal had gone on their recce, beyond was new ground. We waited for the moon to rise fully—it was a strange and eerie place. The silence was oppressive and none of us talked—we were each wrapped up with our own thoughts. I felt excited but apprehensive, we had a long way to go.

The going was hard, through deep unconsolidated snow. We walked in single file, sharing the lead occasionally. The climbing had an air of unreality about it. A few hours before we had been resigned to going back over the Col to fetch fresh supplies, but now here we were plodding silently up a huge moonlit face.

We reached a great snow basin, collecting ground for innumerable avalanches. We tried to quicken the pace but the snow was even deeper. We pressed on to the safety of an ice ridge and reached it just in time. The still night was shattered by a shuddering roar as an avalanche from somewhere ripped across our steps. This was what we had all feared, the horror of being overwhelmed in the night. As the ice dust settled our mood became more relaxed and we began to joke nervously.

Above, the climbing steepened up and we soon came to an ice wall barring the way. I had examined this obstacle through the binoculars and headed for what I knew was the easiest way through. Dougal was in front, however, and he headed to the other end of it. Chris announced that he recalled a way through on the right but it was not found. No-one listened to me and I did not feel like pressing forward without a rope. Dougal began hammering ice pitons in what later revealed itself as the longest, steepest part of the wall. I felt peeved and very cold as I waited.

Chris:

We sat below and shivered. The temperature had been perfect for climbing, the chill keeping us pleasantly cold, but once you stopped the cold slid insidiously up the back of your anorak and through your boots to numb your feet. And yet, in spite of the cold, I could not help being amazed at the sheer desolate beauty of the mountains around us. The moon was now dropping down on to the western horizon, describing a path of light that shone on Shipton's Col. Down the Changabang Glacier, Nanda Devi stood, its huge North Face in shadow, massive yet perfect in its proportions. It looked as big as Everest, silhouetted against the moon.

I could hear Martin's teeth chattering.

'Are you happy?' I asked him.

'Am I fuck! I bloody hate waiting around. I'm sure there's an easy way over there to the left,' he replied.

And at last Dougal pulled over the top of the wall; another long pause while he found a secure anchor for the rope, and then one by one we pulled up the rope, using a single jumar each—desperately strenuous work, made harder from being frozen into immobility.

By the time I got up, Dougal was already out in front again, now on a sloping roof of ice covered by an inadequate coating of snow—a place to go with care, step delicately, fearful, aware of the dark void below.

By this time the grey dawn had lightened the sky; the first rays of the sun had touched the summit of Nanda Devi, crept down its fluted

43. Dougal on the way to the top camp.

44. Crossing a tricky crevasse just below the top camp.

buttresses to play on the lower peaks, and then it even touched Changabang's crest. From the back Changabang presents a crazy knife-edge
snow ridge which clings to a rocky base. It was now lit a brilliant white
in the early morning sun.

Ballu:

Dawn. We see each other's frosted Father Christmas faces—tired and
full of sleep. Where is the bloody col, the prospective camp site? It is
8 a.m. and there is a welcome horizontal shelf in this perpendicular
world. An occasional spindrift of snow. We work like sleep-walkers,
surely and slowly. Tunnels are up, anchored by our ice axes and we are
comfy as fleas—three to a tent now. Brew and sleep, brew and sleep.

Chris:

There was hardly room in the two-man tent for three people, the
primus and all the cooking gear. We lay back, dovetailed into each other,
legs bent to avoid the primus and let its roar lull us into a doze.

There's so much discomfort, so much harsh grinding effort and yet
I've a wonderful feeling of elated anticipation at the prospect of com-
pleting the climb tomorrow. The last few days have welded the team
into a single entity; we seem to be reaching our decisions with very
little discussion, no argument, as if our minds had fused into one
powerful thinking unit. This afternoon Ballu and I had our highest chess

game yet—the standard of play was undoubtedly poor, minds slowed, no doubt, by lack of oxygen.

Ballu:

Stew in the evening. We are now reduced to one spoon in the party and it does for a ladle and community spoon, though Dougal still prefers his rock peg. Flapping of the wind and the occasional avalanche. Silence. Total silence except for our breathing. For once I am so tired that my thoughts also sleep. Wake and try an inconclusive chess game and we share a bag of 'busy' nuts (pine kernels) and shovel stew and mashed potatoes in the evening. Set my mental alarm clock for a 1 a.m. start. Swallow a pill each of vitamin, calcium and iron—and sleep. Ah, the sleep and the deep frozen silence of the hills. Stray thoughts of places, people, unreal and uncertain, dreamlike.

Martin sleeps between Chris and me with his head towards the entrance. It's easier this way for him to get anything from outside and for us to pass him anything from inside the tent. He and Doug, similarly stuck in the other tent, do all the cooking. Crampons and rucksacks lie out in the open. We wear the inner boots inside the sleeping bag so the body heat can dry them. My socks and stockings go into the bag too. The duvet is rolled into a pillow, and the outer boots, gloves and anorak are pushed between the bag and the tent wall. Arrangement of kit before turning in for the night has to be surgical. Rucksacks, ice axes and crampons are outside the tent, near the entrance. You hope not to have to get up for a pee or something more bloody during the night.

4. Six on the summit

Martin:

I did not have too many doubts that we would get up Changabang. We were well positioned at the top camp to make the summit push. The climbing was not hard to the col between Kalanka and Changabang—all we had to do then was get up the long ice ridge. This did not look easy but I was sure we would do it. Even so, we were not in a position to hang around—we had precious little food and the weather, if it went to pattern, could force a premature retreat.

We were a well-knit group. Ballu was going extremely well and I was really getting to like him a lot. I was not quite so confident of Tashi. He was still suffering from severe piles. He had the look of a worried man. I hoped he'd be O.K. He certainly had plenty of determination and was tough—as long as he believed in his own powers. Like all Sherpas he was extremely superstitious and he intimated to me that he was worried about an ill omen.

45. Tashi at the top camp.

Chris:

June 5th. Yesterday was one of the longest, hardest and most satisfying days I have ever had in the mountains. We woke up at one o'clock. Since we had made supper the night before, the others had the job of making breakfast—a brew of tea and a panful of muesli and apple flakes. We were ready to leave by two. It was a brilliant, cold, clear night. What a relief to leave packframes and loads behind—we didn't even take any bivouac gear.

Ballu:

Chris is up; so is Martin. What is the weather like? Crystal clear. Scratching of match sticks and pumping of the stove. Muttering of stove and now a steady hum. To make room for the stove in the tent both Chris and I curl up. Billy of snow melted at night is frozen and will be ready in an hour. Martin wriggles in his bag as he slips his gear on. He hates this. He loves to be ready last. Today that luxury will be mine. Water ready and we eat cold muesli out of the billy. Crampon straps are frozen and fastening crampons is a devil of a chore. Duvet, spare gloves and socks and a torch in the rucksack; descendeur, hammer and short ice axe, share of pegs and rope, a bar of chocolate, a packet of raisins, and amble off into a moon-filled silence.

Chris:

Dougal and I got away first. The only way to the col above us seemed to be straight up—the ice wall barrier was lower there and above it the angle of the slope relented. We climbed a great cone of soft snow to the foot of the wall. It was in the direct line of a continuous torrent of fine powder snow that was pouring down the face from the upper slopes of Kalanka.

I found myself thrust to the front. Perhaps Dougal felt he had done his stint of leading for a while. I teetered on top of the cone of snow, peered round the pendulous lip of the ice overhang that barred the bottom of the wall, and flinched away from the cascade of spindrift that filled my beard, stung my face and slipped down my neck in icy rivulets. I crouched under the shelter of the overhang, caught my breath, reached up and hammered in an ice peg, and then tried to pull up on it, cocking a cramponed boot up by my right ear. It's an energetic move at ground level and sheer, bloody ridiculous for a thirty-nine-year-old at 21 000 feet. I was muttering under my breath—sign of senility. Retreated to the overhang and cringed under its shelter. The rest of the team were now gathered below me. They were muttering too.

'How's it going, Chris?' called Martin. Bloody awful—but I didn't say anything, just returned to the lip, made a mighty heave, levered up, then stood up, my head out of the torrent, I was in balance, bang in another peg, cut a step at full arm's length, a few staccato moves kicking the front points of the crampons into the ice, and I was standing in the step. This was great! I'd forgotten just how good it is to be out lead climbing on hard ice. I forgot all about the others, about everything except the ice, gleaming faintly in front of my nose. I was in complete control, felt the joy of it welling through me. I ran out a hundred feet to where the angle eased and came once more to snow, anchored the rope and called the others up. And as they jumared up I sat and watched the sun brush the summit of Nanda Devi, a magnificent repeat of the sight we'd seen the morning before but this time it seemed even more beautiful, bathed in the rich warm glow of my elation at a pitch well climbed, at having stretched myself to my limits.

Doug:

We lost all our warmth watching Chris tackle the ice bulge with pegs and old-fashioned tension techniques. He swung over the bulge and went out of sight up the hard ice above. Ice chips rained on us and spindrift snow poured over the bulge in windy gusts. Chris fixed his rope and I

46. Tashi and Dougal begin the summit climb up the East Ridge, with the trail from the top camp stamped clear on the slopes behind them.

went up, removing the pegs from the bulge. While shivering at the foot of the pitch, we'd probably all wondered why he'd taken so long and thought we could have done the job better. But the ice above was surprisingly steep and without any snow covering for steps. With the minimum of step-cutting Chris had climbed a hundred feet in the dark with snow whirling about him and in doing so had found the way to the col. One after the other, we climbed up the fixed rope and soloed off to the col.

We stopped in the early morning sun to warm up and dry out and gaze, aghast, at all the peaks and ranges stretching northwards into Tibet. How lucky we were that the weather was fine, that the team was fit, and that our thoughts towards each other were charitable.

Ballu:

Dawn, a beautiful dawn—like the morning of life: no cloud and no wind and a lot of big mountains and some cold. Where on earth are my toes?

An easy-angled snow slope with occasional rock leads to Kalanka Choti—a straight cramponing peak. More soft snow across an easier slope now and we are on the col, on the East Ridge joining Changabang and Kalanka. In the far distance to the north lie blue-covered distances of Tibet, distances of God. Far to the east rises the Kailash massif. A hint of breeze from the north. Good, this.

Dougal:

The way on to Changabang looked difficult, a steep, fluted ridge, while that leading to Kalanka seemed relatively easy. Tempted we were but only momentarily and we quickly turned towards Changabang. The rest of the day was an alternation of leads, always on brittle ice and soft snow with minimal protection.

Ballu:

East Ridge at last. Snow-covered and knife-edge, easy-angled to start but rearing up in a vicious squiggle towards Changabang's 22 520-foot virginal top. We drop our rucksacks and rope up—Tashi, Doug and Dougal on one rope, Chris, Martin and me on another. Rotten, loose snow: fantastic vista of mountains to north and south. Sure, good climbing. Moving one climber at a time is slow. I estimate we will reach the summit by 2 p.m. Straddle the ridge with a boot each down the Bagini Glacier and the Changabang Glacier and somehow keep moving. Initial euphoria is gone. The ropes alternate lead. I finish the roll in my borrowed camera and leave it at that. Six to eighteen inches of soft spongy snow lies over the ice: it does not cake when stamped and gives under weight; some circus balancing and weight distribution over five points and one is up these nasty patches. Unfortunately they come too often—and all bad. Exhausting work. Thirsty now and often out of wind.

Martin:

I led out at first—Ballu and Chris followed. It was a precariously slow business. Sometimes we would climb below the crest, sometimes we would sit astride. There was no room for error. There wasn't time to dig out stances or secure belays, even if it had been possible to find them. Progress was too slow as it was. Fortunately we were working well together and trusted one another and we were all going strongly. The ridge seemed interminable. Light cloud obscured the summit. We cut steps on the really awkward-looking places, thinking of our retreat, until at last it seemed sensible to send two off ahead. So Dougal and Doug bashed out steps, while the four of us climbed behind.

Chris:

We soon discovered that the climbing was more difficult and very much more precarious than we had expected. The crest of the ridge was a genuine knife-edge of none-too-stable snow, clinging to a base of wafery ice. You had the uncomfortable feeling that the entire cockscomb

47. Not far below the summit, Doug protects Dougal's progress along the crest of the ridge.

48. Chris considers the next section of the summit ridge, protected by Ballu and Martin.

could break away with you on it. But the sheer joy of the situation and the climbing was still there. To the north, Changabang's massive wall dropped an incredible 6 000 feet to the Bagini Glacier. Then, as the day stretched out and clouds began to build up around us, a tension crept in. Eleven o'clock, midday, three in the afternoon—we were still below the summit. The ridge twisted tortuously; the anchors were poor; our progress, with six climbers, was inevitably slow; an unwieldy convoy on a high-altitude obstacle course.

Doug:

Shuffling along the rotten, knife-edge arête, breaking track, was slow going, and the other four were able to keep close behind Dougal and me. At about four o'clock Dougal's lead brought him on to the summit ridge. One by one, the others arrived. There was no back-slapping, we were not hale and hearty—in fact, quite the opposite. We were enveloped in a damp, cold mist and there was a long way to go to get back down— twenty roped pitches to the col, then reverse Chris's wall to the tents. We would be doing a continuous night shift.

Chris:

Dougal and Doug seemed near the summit. It was four o'clock and the clouds had rolled in around us. A shout! They were on the top. It was another hour before I got there and all six of us crouched on this little cone of snow. A strange feeling of anti-climax and tension. There was no view, just an occasional glimpse through the clouds of distant peaks merging with more clouds. We were all worried about the descent. We were already tired and there were only a couple of hours of daylight left. Ballu produced his regimental flag. I took a few photographs.

Martin:

We all assembled in a tight huddle on the summit by five. We were not elated—even Doug and Chris were not keen to perform the rituals of summit photography. Our minds were on the descent and the coming darkness.

The summit is nearly always an anti-climax. Once you've knocked it on the head, it loses all its interest, romance, excitement, what have you. We go on a lot about the romance of unknown virgin summits etc. and what do we do? Spoil it by climbing them! Probably the most profound climbing experience for me was our total failure on Cerro Torre. I could not help feeling a deep sadness when it was climbed. Not envy. Sadness.

Ballu:

I draw my anorak tight around my neck and try to control my breathing. My limbs don't seem to believe that there is no more pumping up and up. We stay anchored to the rope and Tashi produces the flags. Pictures in the semi-darkness. Tricolour up for a photograph, hangs limp. Someone has forgotten the Union Jack; my regimental and airborne flags are adopted to represent all the missing flags. Sit amidst swirling cloud for a glimpse of the world of mountains around us.

Dougal:

There was a summit dilemma. We were on a ridge and our high point could have been the summit or it could have been a point a few rope lengths to the south. For the sake of getting down, it wasn't possible for everyone to visit the other point, so Doug and I raced off while the others started the wearing descent. Going very well, we raced up with the rope trailing between us. The new point looked about twenty feet higher but it could have been an optical illusion. Anyway we had settled any possible doubt by climbing both points, and if anyone is still troubled let them work it out by trigonometry.

Turning round we rapidly caught up with the others and joined the descent column.

Ballu:

It is like walking on stilts—long uneven steps down steep slippery snow. Rope after rope, rope after rope. A thousand feet down and we are out of the cloud and into a brilliant moon. Is there someone walking along with me—in step with me? Bright moon and this inner gold? All my loves being with me in this wintry, savage night?

Effortlessly sailing down the mountain, down the mountain, I trip

49. Dougal strikes for the summit as the clouds close in.

50. The last few feet of the climb.

over my crampons and crash into the mountain face—burying my own in the snow. Up and shake myself. Balwant Sandhu sleep-walking as if on a blasted route march in Agra. Rub snow on my eyes and wake up. Crunch and slush, swoosh and rustle. And down and down into the silence for my body has withered away and I and my soul walk hand in hand into the land of sunshine. And then I flounder, like an ice cube in a whisky tumbler and shake myself awake. Too bad this. I begin a game with the alphabet and my unit: after each letter I try to remember as many of my NCOs whose names begin with that letter. I am awake all right but keep losing the letter. Bone dry and parched, we sleep-walk down the ridge. The traverse above the col was bad in the morning. And now? It is vile.

Martin:

We climbed down as fast as possible but it was still a painfully slow business. Chris had been a bit stroppy on the way up, ordering Tashi and Ballu about—'For God's sake, Ballu, clip on the fucking rope, will you!'—'Hurry up, Tashi, sit astride the ridge,' forgetting about his piles.

It was now my turn to shout the odds at Chris who was coming down too slowly for my liking. I was seething with impatience—at this rate we would have to bivouac.

We got on to the long level section of the ridge. Chris favoured dropping down on to a vague shelf along which we would progress more quickly. He couldn't find a safe anchor so he buggered around. He finally found one thirty feet below the ridge and roped off down. The rope didn't reach the shelf. I groaned and soloed off while he jumared laboriously back up. Ballu followed me but Doug burst out in a rage and so he remained, roped up. I traversed quickly and easily. The steps had now frozen perfectly and I reached easy ground as the light faded. The others followed slowly. I could hear their progress in the dark. I waited for them, guided them down the last bit and went off by myself again. The others soon caught me up. I took a rope from them, fixed a little abseil, and once more shot off and down the easy snow slopes. I fixed the last abseil into camp, re-erected the tents and got a brew on. It was ten o'clock when the others arrived. It had been a twenty-two-hour day.

Later we came to realise just how lucky we had been—the summit day was the only day of the expedition without bad weather.

Doug:

Having knocked off the second summit, marginally higher than the other, Dougal and I hurtled back down the ridge on the heels of the others.

The mist evaporated from our mountain but all above was a blanket of grey cloud. The mountains of the Garhwal had lost their sparkle and now looked exceedingly sombre. Over in secret Tibet, however, the sky was a pale watery blue and the sun lit up a patchwork of fields and rolling downland between purple mountain ranges. Now I can recall that startling scene more than any other on the whole trip. For I gazed out from the Changabang snow arête totally absorbed. There was none of the usual relating the scene to others I remembered because I had never seen anything quite like that particular backcloth. I was too tired to consider that none of the peaks out there had important names, that I might write about them, that there was the forbidden, mysterious land of Tibet, for I was seeing the scene as a child lost among it. For once I was not a separate performer—geographer, mountaineer, admirer or whatever, using the mountains—but felt to be actually part of them. The feeling did not last long, for soon the dark closed in and we were left to stumble and curse, groping for our previous footsteps.

Chris:

The way down wasn't as bad as I had expected for the snow had been packed down by our ascent and had consolidated in the cool of the evening. It was dark, however, by the time we reached the end of the ice ridge. I was the last man off it, feeling down with my booted feet in the gloom for invisible steps—extra cautious at this last, steep step. We had a short climb to get back over the col, and this, more than anything, brought home just how tired we were. It was now a perfect starlight

51. 'We all assembled in a tight huddle on the summit by five. We were not elated.'

night, with the barest breath of wind, and yet it was all we could do to put one foot in front of the other. Had the weather broken, had we been fighting our way back in the teeth of a storm, I wonder if we should have had the strength left to get back.

We were over the col, dropping down the other side; reached a short bad step; Doug tried to reverse it, but it was too steep; we got the rope out, anchored it, and went down hand over hand. Ballu, over confident, tried to go too fast, slipped, let go and fell in a heap at the bottom, but fortunately stopped and was unhurt. Down and down to the top of the ice wall I had led up a hundred years before—that morning. I stayed behind to be the last one down and to pull down the abseil rope. There was a strange satisfaction in sitting crouched in the cold, secured to the anchor piton, gazing across at Changabang's cockscomb, brilliantly lit in the light of the moon. I had a feeling of total peace with myself, of having done my utmost. I had a feeling of strong affection for every single member of our little group. Changabang might not have been the biggest or the hardest unclimbed peak in the world but it had given us three days of intensity of effort and living that would sustain us for a long time.

'The rope's clear,' called Doug, and it was my turn to go down. I slid down the rope, grabbed one end and carefully backed down the snow-covered ice to the two tents. The primus stove was roaring. Ballu and Martin were already in their sleeping bags. I struggled with frozen crampon straps, heaved off my boots and crawled in behind them to lie impatient, mouth parched, for our first brew or drink for twenty hours. That night we didn't cook any food, just drank and drank, talked a little, wondering at the greatness of the day we had just completed.

Dougal:

By Himalayan standards it had been a long day but I did not feel any more tired than I would if I'd spent the same length of time out in the Alps. I wonder if continuous exposure to altitude over the years makes for better acclimatisation? Certainly, I was having no problems on this trip. Mentally we were all in fine shape. Though there was a vague unease about the descent in most of our minds we wandered through in fine style, leaving behind us, with Changabang, all our immediate mountaineering urges.

Chris:

The rest of the descent was an anti-climax. The day dawned dull and cloudy and we were ready to leave about nine-thirty. We were lucky it was a dull day for this meant the snow was that much safer. We got back to the camp at the foot of the Face at about midday, put up the tents and had a magnificent stew cooked by Martin. Then we dozed for the rest of the day until about five-thirty—time to start on the final leg, the fifteen-hundred-foot grind to the Shipton Col.

Down with the tentage, and then the only dispute that marred those days. It wasn't serious but it emphasised, perhaps, the different backgrounds of the Indians and ourselves. We had more gear at the camp than we could possibly carry—Ballu wanted to get everything he possibly could back over the Col for all forms of mountaineering equipment are desperately expensive and almost impossible to obtain in India. We, on the other hand, spoilt by several expeditions-worth of free gear, were happy to leave the lot behind. Wasteful, over-affluent Westerners! We disputed how much to carry, and then Tashi put us to shame, exhausted as he was, by loading himself with an extra rope. We all took a little extra communal equipment.

The walk up to the Col was long drawn out, twenty paces, a rest and another twenty paces, but slowly the distance shortened. I was the last up, but had a wait of half an hour before the others had all started down. Tashi was immediately in front of me. It had now started to snow and the fixed rope dropped down the snow-plastered walls, now dimming fast in the evening gloom. We couldn't see across the glacier to our final haven. Tashi started down the first length of rope. It was lucky it was a short stretch, for on the change-over he got himself irretrievably tangled so that he could move neither up nor down. I tried to explain to him what to do, shouted and yelled at him, and finally, using my jumar as a safeguard, climbed down the rope to try to free him. By dint of pulling and hauling I finally got him free and he was able to continue down. I followed, plunging down through the milling spindrift in the dark of the night. The way back across the glacier was interminable but at last we saw a light, heard voices, and we were back at Base Camp, to hot drinks, the warm welcome of DJ, and most precious of all, the first batch of letters from home we had had on the expedition.

8. Home Thoughts

ON THE WAY to the mountain all the climbers, and Chris more than anyone, had been full of plans for further conquest if the Changabang climb went quickly and well. But Changabang proved enough for everyone. They returned to Base Camp drained of mountaineering ambition for the time being. Perhaps the fact that letters from home were waiting for them there—the first letters of the expedition—dispersed the last lingering twitches of any urge to carry on climbing. Certainly, they packed up promptly and set off home.

The four British climbers were all married men. Every expedition involves a separation—for at least four weeks and usually for considerably longer, two or three months. For the men there is no problem. They are doing, in the current jargon, their thing, satisfying their appetites for adventure, enjoying new scenes and making new friends and meeting new challenges. Expedition life may not always be entirely pleasant but it is all-absorbing.

It is very different for the wives. The only change in their scene is the absence of the man of the house. They must take his responsibilities as well as their own—with the extra ever-present worry that he might be killed or badly injured.

What do the wives think about it? How do they take it? After some initial reluctance three of the Changabang grass-widows agreed to talk.

The odd wife out was Annie Haston, Dougal's wife. The Hastons have not been married as long as the others. Unlike the others, they have no children. Annie does a full-time job as a nurse in Switzerland. When I wrote asking for her thoughts, the reply came from Dougal:

We both feel that expedition time is great. It gives us both time to do the things we want, outside of the things we enjoy doing together. Most of my travelling is mountain orientated, whereas Annie likes to visit historic cities and sunny islands by the sea or go trekking. In close relationships such as marriage it really helps to have separation periods. I refuse to believe that people can live in close contact for twelve months a year and still have some freshness or interest left in the relationship. That's the way we work, anyway. Maximum freedom.

Jan Scott

Hank:

Jan Scott was the first wife to reply and the only one to put her feelings down in writing and it was what she said that encouraged the other two to talk. The Scotts have two children, Michael who was eleven at the time of Changabang and a very young daughter, Martha. Doug has been a compulsive expedition absentee throughout their married life. After Changabang, for example, he was at home in Nottingham for one week, then went off to lead the English contingent to the international climbing meet in the Pamirs.

Jan:

People usually ask if I'm scared that Doug is going to get killed. Well, I just never worry about that possibility because there's no point in it. If he's going to get the chop—to use the pungent climbing expression— my worrying isn't going to stop an accident, and I feel that if Doug is killed on a mountain then an accident is what it will be. He's a very strong man with immense reserves of strength which he can call on during a long seige. I know he has no death wish—that he will push himself to the limit but not beyond it. If you have had as many hours of mountain exposure as Doug has without being killed, it means you are a very careful mountaineer, and a lucky one.

One of the hardest things I have had to come to terms with is his determination to get to the mountains. At first it did seem to be a rejection of me and the kids, the home side of his life. And practically all the trips he has made have meant a degree of financial hardship. This, together with leaving me with the responsibility of the kids for twenty-four hours a day, could easily overwhelm our relationship.

When he's away I become almost too independent. I find it very hard to accept Doug sharing my life when he comes back from any trip longer than six weeks. I've organised myself very nicely, thank you. In fact, I don't really need him any more. It's a form of self-preservation for me, so that if Doug does get killed then I don't have a fantastic adjustment to make—I've already adjusted to his not being around. But mostly it stops the feeling of desperate need and loneliness and rejection that I would feel if I did not cut him out of my life.

I realised I would have to do something about it during his first trip to the Atlas in the year we were married because I seemed to spend the whole time feeling desperately unhappy and in fact I literally just about took to my bed with missing him so much. It took quite a few trips for us to realise what had happened—this adjustment of mine. It's the weeks immediately after his return that are always the most traumatic for us. It's very hard for me to accept him as part of my life again. He comes back panting to be a husband, father, etc. again, and I sort of look at him and say, 'Who is this guy?'

On the positive side, we are very lucky we are both doing things that interest and involve us so much. I get as much of a kick out of my job as Doug does from his climbing. The knowledge that I'm good at teaching, especially with difficult children, gives me great confidence. I don't mean this in a chauvinist women's lib way, but simply that it's good for me to know I can exist as a contributing person in a life outside of Doug. It means he respects me, too, so when I'm screeching at him because he's going off for three months and hasn't paid the phone bill, he doesn't think of me simply as the idiot wife. It also helps to be able to get out of the house and go to work and forget the phone bill. Otherwise I would sit at home, worrying like mad, with all my upper working class values knocking about in my head.

As for the kids, well Martha's too young to understand what's happening yet. It was a big strain on Michael because he was young at the time when I was having a lot of trouble coming to terms with a guy who would spend 99.9 per cent of his time in and around climbing. But now Michael is beginning to reap the rewards. He travels quite a lot with Doug—he's been to the States and to Nepal in the last few years. So he's getting something back now instead of just giving all the time in the form of having to manage without Doug as a father, then having to accept him back. But these are troubles that confront the children of sailors and reps and all kinds of people who are away a lot. I really feel that if I am generally happy and at peace while Doug is away, then the kids are too. The dog feels it worst—poor old Strider gets very distressed and fussy when Doug's away.

So on the whole I don't resent Doug's going away too much and I don't worry madly about him, although I confess to an immense feeling of relief when I hear that he's off the mountain and on his way home. I've been known to leap madly round the school hugging the other teachers—much to the amazement of the kids.

Wendy Bonington

Hank:

Wendy Bonington has some things in common with Jan Scott—two children, Daniel and Rupert; a husband who is an obsessional mountaineer; and a working interest—in art, book illustration, picture editing—that can operate independently of her husband. She has had to suffer one uniquely nightmarish experience. In 1966 their first child, Conrad, at that time their only child, was drowned in a stream in the Lake District. Chris was exploring in Ecuador when it happened, and Wendy endured more than a week of solitary grief before he could get back to England. Wendy does not go to airports to see him off, nor does she go at the end of an expedition to welcome him back. Nor, for that matter, do the other wives. She likes to help afterwards, organising and selecting photographs for lectures, articles, books, but she keeps shyly clear of any publicity fuss or lionising.

Wendy:

Chris and I married because, among other things, we get a great deal of pleasure from each other's company, enjoy doing things together and thoroughly enjoy doing nothing in particular together. However, he has this recurring urge to go off climbing or adventuring, and I need periods of time to be solitary, alone and undisturbed with my thoughts.

When he goes off on some expedition, Chris is creating the situation in a positive way—he chooses the time and length of time and has a specific aim. I have to adapt to this, whether I feel like it or not. It may not be a convenient time for me to make the best use of it—things like moving house or some such domestic unheaval, problems of coping with the children in the holidays can mean that I have a lot to organise alongside whatever I want to do, and he will sometimes return to a rather frustrated wife.

On a really big expedition the pre-trip organisation (which also entails Chris's absence and preoccupation, rushing around trying to make enough money for our basic living while he's away) and all the worries that go with it, can put quite a strain on the whole family. Chris always has terrible last-minute doubts about his exploits and thrashes about like a wounded whale, so I can be quite glad to see the expedition go at last, knowing his doubts will disappear once he gets going. I can then enjoy settling into my own personal tempo. A night person, I like to sleep in the morning as long as the kids will allow, whereas Chris will often leap out of bed, horribly bright at four in the morning, and subside in the early evening just when I'm getting into my stride.

Chris, too, seems to be able to concentrate under any conditions, amid any amount of noise, though he does need quiet for creative writing. For me it's difficult to concentrate unless I find myself an environment that is undistracting and I must get away from noise, especially the presence of people. If I want to paint when Chris is at home I have to lock myself away in my workroom. He used to get a bit hurt about this but understands now.

We're both very emotional people and he gets very homesick almost as soon as he's left the country. He writes lots of letters and on Everest recorded a diary of his thoughts and feelings, and stories for the kids too, on cassette tapes.

Physically, of course, one misses out when apart. We get a tremendous amount just from the awareness of the other being close by, even if we are both totally preoccupied in doing different things. Physical touch we need between us—hand-holding or just a foot touching and when we are together we tend to gravitate physically, and sleep incredibly tangled up. When he's away one of the worst moments of the day is getting into bed by myself.

After he has been away a while, although the situation strengthens my feeling of independence, inside me seems too steely, too cold-brittle, and I long for the warmth of Chris's companionship. Like a plant that has withered for lack of the right attention. I take quite a time to fully revive and adjust when he does come home.

Basically I am enormously relieved once he is back home, content that our family unit is whole again, but I feel the intrusion of the things that tend to go with his return—the telephone ringing non-stop, the hustle of closing down the expedition and the demands this makes on both of us. The children also are desperately needing to catch up on having a Dad around.

It's difficult to know whether they worry about what their father's up to when he's absent. Now at ages five and seven they pick up things from general conversation you don't realise and I'm sure other children at school put ideas into their heads. They come out with some pretty straight questions sometimes; 'What if Daddy gets killed?'; and once when he seemed a long time getting back home—'Is Daddy dead?'. Mostly, though, they come out with 'I want Daddy', just when I'm having to tell them off about something. The round-the-clock responsibility of coping with them is hard for me. I often feel so inadequate in this role and actively worry about them much more than I do about Chris.

I am not a natural worrier, being basically optimistic, but hate being continually asked if I worry about Chris when he's away. It's a bit like walking a tightrope. You've got to be totally aware of the realities of a situation which is completely beyond your control and being asked if you worry is like being asked to look down; it certainly doesn't help and makes keeping your balance that much more difficult.

Changabang, though, was enjoyed by us all. It was a short trip by Himalayan standards and the absence of hullabaloo kept the usual stresses for me at a manageable level. We were moving back to the Cumberland fells, which was very important to me, and although we were having to live in a small caravan the whole time Chris was away as the conversion to our cottage was not yet complete, it was great to see the kids totally absorbed in their new surroundings. The weather was marvellous and it was like being on holiday. We all enjoyed ourselves in our different ways and reunited content in each other's happiness.

But you can't have jam on it all the time. I think our way of life, for us, is rich and challenging. It expands and strengthens us as individuals and tests and deepens our relationship.

Maggie Boysen

Hank:

Finally, the Boysens. They have one little girl who is too young to have much idea what is going on.

Maggie:

I don't in the least resent Martin's going off on expeditions. I know it sounds strange, even unnatural, but it's true. For one thing, I've done some climbing and I know how fascinating it can be. It's a very important part of Martin's life and I'm happy just knowing he's doing what he wants to do. I knew exactly what I was in for when I married him. He'd been off climbing every weekend ever since I first met him and I knew I wasn't going to change him. I can't be everything in his life and I accept that. And in a way it's not quite the same for me as for the others. Martin has not done as much expedition-going as the others, at least until this past year and when we were first married—he was away for four months then in South America and I had a terrible time, didn't know how to cope with it at all and felt very unhappy and insecure.

But I learned to cope with it and in some ways now I adore it when he's away, especially in the first few weeks. It's like the others really, I can organise my life to suit myself, do the things that I want to do. I'm studying hard to become a member of the Institute of Biology and I can get on with that in peace. I read lots of novels and do loads of gardening. I thoroughly enjoy not being buggered about by Martin. He's a very fussy, fastidious person in some ways and when he's home I seem to spend a lot of time messing about with trivial things just to keep him quiet—things like disinfecting the rubbish bin. When he's away I can be as sluttish as I like. And I have so much more time. When he's home Martin likes me to be with him, sit with him, even if he's only watching some boring programme on television. And I do it even though I'd rather go to another room and read.

It is a strengthening thing, to be left to cope on your own. I have got to know myself a lot better through it. I feel more able and independent. I know I can cope. I'm not frightened of life any more.

It's all right, as I said, for a few weeks. But after that I do begin to feel lonely and start to miss his companionship. I think we have a very special relationship, Martin and me. He's the only person I know who is exactly on my wave-length. We react to many things in precisely the same way, have the same sense of humour. Very often when something or someone is going on we catch each other's eye and know exactly what the other is thinking. I get to miss that very much. And, of course, you really miss him when something goes seriously wrong. When Martin was on Torre Egge our little girl's hand was smashed in a car door. I missed Martin very badly then.

I worry a great deal that he might be killed or badly hurt. I find it hard to believe that Jan can seal her feelings off like that and force herself not to worry. It's not just a matter of having confidence in the bloke. I know Martin's a good and careful and experienced climber and won't do anything stupid or suicidal. But the statistics are horrifying and the dangers in the big mountains are so blind, so unpredictable that he could be killed by sheer bloody bad luck however careful or skilful he was. That's what terrifies me. I know this can happen to Martin—it has happened to many of our friends—and I worry badly about it and have bad dreams that he's been killed.

One thing, though, I don't lose weight when he's away. When he's at home he won't let me eat a lot because he likes me to keep slim. So when he's away I get at all the fattening things I love—cakes and honey buns, everything that's bad for me—and let myself go.

9. Conclusions

IT WAS A SUCCESSFUL expedition. Not completely successful because the original intention was to climb Changabang by the West Ridge and gain experience in hard rock climbing at Himalayan altitudes, and in the event the mountain was conquered by its South-East ridge, on snow and ice. Nonetheless, the objective was not easy, yet six men gained the summit and got down safely again. No-one was killed and no-one was badly injured. And there were no serious rows. The climbers came down with old friendships strengthened and new ones, between the British and the Indian climbers, firmly based.

Nor was it, by modern Himalayan standards, an expensive expedition. The total cost worked out at about £7000, which is about one-fifth of the cost of the 1970 Annapurna expedition and only just over one-tenth of the cost of Chris' Everest attempt in 1972. Even so, it is salutary to compare the price of Changabang with that of the exploration of the Nanda Devi basin in 1934. Tilman and Shipton were away from England for seven months and were travelling in the mountains for five months, and when it was all over Shipton worked out their total expenditure, from leaving England to returning, came to £143. 10s. each. The value of sterling has, of course, declined in the intervening forty years, but it seems as if there has also been some decline in the hardihood of our adventurers.

In the end, then, what had been gained? Another of the earth's high points had fallen beneath man's all-conquering boots. Ten men had enjoyed a six-week break that was often pleasant and always interesting. The British had extended their experience of hard going at high altitude and the Indian sumiteers had learned something of modern techniques. And it had been shown that climbers of differing nationalities and races, although with a common language, could share the rigours of camping and climbing and decision-making in a friendly spirit.

Ballu:

The climb was good. What I find particularly flattering is surmounting the summit at a human level. We climbed not as climbers from two nations but as a team. On an expedition it is always tricky to subdue individual ambitions, vanities and idiosyncrasies. Initially, the Indian members were sometimes peeved at having more than their share of the work of getting the expedition to the Base Camp. But we spoke the language and the British members did not. And once on the mountain everyone did his best without a thought of his nationality. In climbing Changabang and returning as friends, we scored a 'right' and a 'left'.

I had been excited about the trip ever since it was first conceived, during the international rock climbing camp in Kashmir in June '73. The excitement of climbing a tough Himalayan mountain was matched by the prospect of using the latest climbing gear and techniques in the company of first-rate climbers.

I and the Indian members feel the trip was great, worth every penny, every drop of sweat. There is a bit of Hermam Buhl in most climbers. Personally I enjoyed it to the limit. It stretched us and was not tame.

To begin with I was doubtful whether the shared leadership would work. We had toyed with the idea of having an Indian responsible for getting the expedition to Base Camp and having the British leader in sole charge on the mountain. For obvious reasons, this idea was rejected and we decided on a shared leadership throughout. And this worked. Chris and I were able to work together mainly because of the quality of the climbers, Indian and British. I can remember few expeditions—single-nation expeditions even—that had more bonhomie, more rapport among the climbers.

Chris and I were able to discuss expedition matters dispassionately, though sometimes we did not agree. Two-nation groups and shared leadership do create problems, but they can be resolved with common sense. All climbers should have the same standard equipment, and they should have common menus. And it is helpful if, before the big effort, they can work together on bouldering or acclimatisation climbs, on mixed ropes, to get the measure of each other's abilities.

Chris:

The intensity of the summit experience can be gauged by the fact that none of us were keen to do any more climbing when we got back to Base Camp. All of us felt that Changabang had been enough, that we had been so lucky with the weather, catching the only fine day of the entire trip, and lucky in avoiding the very real objective dangers. We felt we had used up our stock of good fortune. We were as drained as one is after climbing a much higher mountain, the effect, no doubt, of a series of unusually long days of high-altitude effort. We were sated with climbing and mountains and longed for home. And yet now, back home, I am sure that every single one of us would love to return to try the next challenge on Changabang—the South Ridge, with its sharp gendarmes and ice-veined cracks.

The friendship we built up with the Indian members is something that will last a long time, much longer than the ephemeral satisfaction one gets from bagging another summit. I would love to go back to the Nanda Devi sanctuary, and would happily go with any of the five men who shared those few exacting and exciting days on Changabang.

Hank:

By mid-June the whole party had dispersed. DJ the doctor surprised everyone by going off to get married; he had not said a word about it during the expedition. Tashi and Ujagar returned to teach climbing to the next generation of Indian mountaineers. Kiran and Ballu went back to jumping out of aeroplanes in the interests of national security.

Doug rushed home ahead of the others to get ready to rush off again to the Pamirs. The other three enjoyed some intensive Indian hospitality in Delhi and Agra before flying home. Dougal went straight to the Alps to help Clint Eastwood shoot some hair-raising sequences on the Eiger North Wall and Martin joined them briefly. Chris plunged immediately into planning his next big venture, his second attempt to conquer Everest by the South-West Face route in the post-monsoon season of 1975 with a team including Dougal and Martin and Doug.

A letter from Ballu ended with the words, 'After every mountain I find it a bloody job getting used to the humdrum of living at sea level. So God help me!'